First World War
and Army of Occupation
War Diary
France, Belgium and Germany

47 DIVISION
Divisional Troops
Divisional Ammunition Column
20 March 1915 - 30 March 1919

WO95/2718/4

The Naval & Military Press Ltd
www.nmarchive.com
Published in association with The National Archives

Published by

The Naval & Military Press Ltd

Unit 10 Ridgewood Industrial Park,

Uckfield, East Sussex,

TN22 5QE England

Tel: +44 (0) 1825 749494

www.naval-military-press.com

www.nmarchive.com

This diary has been reprinted in facsimile from the original. Any imperfections are inevitably reproduced and the quality may fall short of modern type and cartographic standards.

© Crown Copyright
Images reproduced by permission of The National Archives, London, England, 2015.

Contents

Document type	Place/Title	Date From	Date To
Heading	WO95/2718/4 47 Div. Div. Amm. Column Mar 15-Mar 19		
Heading	47th Division 47th Divl. Ammn Colmn. Mar 1915-Mar 1919		
Heading	Div. Ammn Col. 47th (London) Division Vol I 20.3-30.4.15		
War Diary	Waterloo	20/03/1915	20/03/1915
War Diary	Havre	21/03/1915	22/03/1915
War Diary	Mazenghem	22/03/1915	26/03/1915
War Diary	Lozenghem	27/03/1915	13/04/1915
War Diary	Annezin	14/04/1915	30/04/1915
Heading	47th Divl. Ammn Col. Vol II 1-30.5.15		
War Diary	Annezin	01/05/1915	23/05/1915
War Diary	Fouquereuil	23/05/1915	30/05/1915
War Diary	Annezin	22/05/1915	23/05/1915
Heading	47th Division 47th Divl. Ammn. Col. Vol III 30.6.15		
Miscellaneous	A Form Messages And Signals		
War Diary	Fouquereuil	01/06/1915	02/06/1915
War Diary	Vaudricourt	02/06/1915	09/06/1915
War Diary	Bois Des Dames	09/06/1915	30/06/1915
Miscellaneous	A Form Messages And Signals		
Heading	47th Divl. Ammn. Col. Vol IV From 1st To 31st July 1915		
War Diary	Bois Des Dames	01/07/1915	31/07/1915
Heading	47th Divl. Ammn. Col. Aug-Sep 1915 Vol V		
War Diary	Bois Des Dames D26.d.1.6	11/08/1915	19/08/1915
War Diary	Bois Des Dames	02/09/1915	02/09/1915
War Diary	Labuissiere	05/09/1915	29/10/1915
Heading	War Diary Divisional Ammunition Column. (47th Division) September 1915		
War Diary	Haillicourt	01/09/1915	30/09/1915
Heading	Ammn. Col. 47th Div. Nov Vol VI		
War Diary	Labuissiere	01/11/1915	17/11/1915
War Diary	Auchel	18/11/1915	29/11/1915
Heading	47th Div. Ammn. Col. Dec Vol VII		
War Diary	Auchel	01/12/1915	01/12/1915
War Diary	Liettres	02/12/1915	03/12/1915
War Diary	Auchel	04/12/1915	14/12/1915
War Diary	Gosnay	16/12/1915	18/12/1915
War Diary	Hesdigneul	19/12/1915	25/12/1915
Heading	47th Divl. Ammn. Col. Jan Vol VIII		
War Diary	Hesdigneul	01/01/1916	30/01/1916
Miscellaneous	47 Div Am Col Vol IX		
War Diary	Hesdigneul	02/02/1916	17/02/1916
War Diary	Auchel	21/02/1916	29/02/1916
War Diary	In The Field	01/03/1916	23/03/1916
Heading	47 Div. Am. Col. Vol X		
War Diary	In The Field	25/03/1916	30/03/1916
War Diary	Magnicourt	01/04/1916	20/05/1916
War Diary	Caucourt	21/05/1916	26/05/1916

War Diary	Magnicourt	27/05/1916	16/06/1916
War Diary	Barlin	17/06/1916	29/06/1916
Heading	47th Divisional Artillery 47th Divisional Ammunition Column R.F.A. July 1916		
War Diary	Barlin	01/07/1916	26/07/1916
War Diary	Bruay	26/07/1916	30/07/1916
War Diary	Vacqueries Le Boucq	31/07/1916	31/07/1916
Heading	47th Divisional Artillery 47th Divisional Ammunition Column R.F.A. August 1916		
War Diary	Vacqueries-Le-Boucq	01/08/1916	01/08/1916
War Diary	Occoches	01/08/1916	05/08/1916
War Diary	Tollent	05/08/1916	10/08/1916
War Diary	Berneuil	10/08/1916	11/08/1916
War Diary	Naours	11/08/1916	12/08/1916
War Diary	Agnicourt	12/08/1916	14/08/1916
War Diary	Albert	14/08/1916	16/09/1916
War Diary	Becourt Wood	17/09/1916	08/10/1916
War Diary	Mametz	09/10/1916	13/10/1916
War Diary	Becourt	14/10/1916	14/10/1916
War Diary	Behencourt	15/10/1916	15/10/1916
War Diary	Moulliens	16/10/1916	16/10/1916
War Diary	Orville	17/10/1916	17/10/1916
War Diary	Vacquerie Le Boucq	18/10/1916	18/10/1916
War Diary	Anvin	19/10/1916	19/10/1916
War Diary	Therouanne	20/10/1916	20/10/1916
War Diary	St Jan-Ter-Biezen	22/10/1916	22/10/1916
War Diary	Busseboom	23/10/1916	31/05/1917
War Diary	Sheet 28 H 13 C	00/05/1917	11/06/1917
War Diary	La Clytte	13/06/1917	08/07/1917
War Diary	Dickebusch Lake	09/07/1917	19/07/1917
War Diary	La Clytte	22/07/1917	21/08/1917
War Diary	Boeschepe	22/08/1917	24/08/1917
War Diary	Reninghelst	29/08/1917	30/08/1917
War Diary	Hoograaf	02/09/1917	11/09/1917
War Diary	Mount Noir	13/09/1917	30/09/1917
War Diary	Ronge Croix	01/10/1917	01/10/1917
War Diary	Boesinghem	02/10/1917	04/10/1917
War Diary	Anzin	05/10/1917	08/10/1917
War Diary	Anzin St Aubin	09/10/1917	31/10/1917
War Diary	Anzin Near Arras	01/11/1917	14/11/1917
War Diary	Ohlain	21/11/1917	22/11/1917
War Diary	Wanquetin	23/11/1917	23/11/1917
War Diary	Sapignes	24/11/1917	24/11/1917
War Diary	Bus	25/11/1917	25/11/1917
War Diary	Vallulart Wood	27/11/1917	09/12/1917
War Diary	Bus	09/12/1917	07/01/1918
War Diary	Dernancourt St Gratien	08/01/1918	10/01/1918
War Diary	Pont Noyelle	12/01/1918	28/02/1918
Heading	War Diary 47th Divisional Ammunition Column R.F.A. March 1918		
War Diary	Pont Noyelles	01/03/1918	03/03/1918
War Diary	Dernancourt	05/03/1918	25/03/1918
War Diary	Fonquevillers	26/03/1918	26/03/1918
War Diary	Gaudiempre	26/03/1918	28/03/1918
War Diary	Souastre	29/03/1918	30/03/1918
War Diary	Equancourt	21/03/1918	22/03/1918

War Diary	Le Mesnil	23/03/1918	23/03/1918
War Diary	Le Transloy	23/03/1918	24/03/1918
War Diary	Longueval	24/03/1918	24/03/1918
War Diary	Trones Wood	24/03/1918	24/03/1918
War Diary	Contalmaison	24/03/1918	24/03/1918
War Diary	Pozieres	24/03/1918	25/04/1918
War Diary	Meaulte	25/04/1918	26/04/1918
War Diary	Senlis	26/04/1918	26/04/1918
War Diary	Vauchelles	26/04/1918	26/04/1918
War Diary	Dernancourt	22/03/1918	31/03/1918
Heading	War Diary 47th Divisional Ammunition Column April 1918		
War Diary	Couin	02/04/1918	06/05/1918
War Diary	Gezaincourt	07/05/1918	07/05/1918
War Diary	St Ouen	08/05/1918	08/05/1918
War Diary	Bray-Les-Mareuil	09/05/1918	21/05/1918
War Diary	Bourdon	22/05/1918	22/05/1918
War Diary	Beaucourt	23/05/1918	30/06/1918
War Diary	Longpre Les Amiens	01/07/1918	13/07/1918
War Diary	Longpre	13/07/1918	13/07/1918
War Diary	Beaucourt	14/07/1918	31/07/1918
Heading	47th Divl. Artillery 47th Divisional Ammunition Column August 1918		
War Diary	Beaucourt	01/08/1918	24/08/1918
War Diary	Warloy Albert	25/08/1918	30/08/1918
War Diary	Fricourt	31/08/1918	03/09/1918
War Diary	Montauban	04/09/1918	07/09/1918
War Diary	Mericourt L'Abbe	07/09/1918	09/09/1918
War Diary	Ames	10/09/1918	20/09/1918
War Diary	Marest	20/09/1918	26/09/1918
War Diary	Anvin	27/09/1918	29/09/1918
War Diary	Ames	01/10/1918	01/10/1918
War Diary	Robecq	02/10/1918	02/10/1918
War Diary	La Gorgue	03/10/1918	03/10/1918
War Diary	Laventie	04/10/1918	17/10/1918
War Diary	St Floris	18/10/1918	23/10/1918
War Diary	Bout Deville	25/10/1918	25/10/1918
War Diary	Haubourdin	26/10/1918	26/10/1918
War Diary	Le Breucq	28/10/1918	31/10/1918
War Diary	Breucq	01/11/1918	10/11/1918
War Diary	Fourcruix	11/11/1918	15/11/1918
War Diary	Louvil	16/11/1918	27/11/1918
War Diary	Fournes	28/11/1918	30/11/1918
War Diary	Chocques	04/12/1918	30/03/1919

WO95/2718 (4)

47 Div
Div. Amm. Column
Mar '15 — Mar '19

47TH DIVISION

47TH DIVL AMMN COLMN.
MAR 1915-MAR 1919

121/5254

Div. Comm. in Chief. 47th (London) Division

Vol I 20.3 — 30.4.15

Army Form C. 2118.

WAR DIARY
or
INTELLIGENCE SUMMARY

(Erase heading not required.)

Instructions regarding War Diaries and Intelligence Summaries are contained in F. S. Regs., Part II. and the Staff Manual respectively. Title pages will be prepared in manuscript.

2nd London Division Ammunition Column
(R.F.A.)(T.F.)

Hour, Date, Place	Summary of Events and Information	Remarks and references to Appendices
12.40 am 20th March 15 Tortotes	Entrained 241 H.D. horses 46 vehicles 4 18 Officers train on 8 trains for SOUTHAMPTON. Arrived SOUTHAMPTON from 3.30 am to 3.30 pm and embarked for HAVRE on transports ARCHIMEDES and EMPRESS QUEEN - before embarking 39 H.D. horses were cast by A.D.V.S. for influenza and 150 H.D. remounts were known to complete establishment of 352 H.D. and on return to replace one sent, making 46 Riders, on a total of 400 horses.	JK
11 am. 21st March 15 HAVRE.	Commenced to disembark at 11 am. Lorry arrived at HAVRE at 7 am. The Column entrained at 11.15 pm in four trains - 19 H.D. horses were left behind through having been taken away in error among a draft of horses for Remounts.	JK
22nd March	Passed through MONTEROL BOSCHY at 6 am. ABBEVILLE - STOMER at 6 pm. horses twice watered and then timed fed. arrived BERGUETTE at 8.30 pm first train - the others following	JK
1.30 am 22/23 March 15 MAZENGHEM	Marched to MAZENGHEM - "I" Section arriving 1.30 am. and the remainder of the Column up to 10.30 am - Considerable difficulty with remount horses from SOUTHAMPTON as Anglais had to be taken from wagons & fitted on hocks as best possible. Also consequences a number of articles of material first left at HAVRE and BERGUETTE	JK

1247 W 3299 200,000 (E) 8/14 J.B.C. & A. Forms/C. 2118/11.

Army Form C. 2118.

WAR DIARY
or
INTELLIGENCE SUMMARY
(Erase heading not required.)

Hour, Date, Place	Summary of Events and Information	Remarks and references to Appendices
11 am. 23 March '15 MAZENGHEM	Brig. Gen'l Col. WRAY - C.R.A. 2nd LONDON DIVL ARTY inspected the Horse Lines.	J/F
24 March '15	Rain fell all day - and with little room to shift horse lines they were soon deep in mud - the horses standing in considerable discomfort.	J/F
25 "	Rain still falling without intermission with piercing N.E. wind. Horses suffering from exposure - especially those which are clipped out. Gunner ENGLAND D. sent to hosp. of minimum importance.	J/F
26 "	Three horses died in the night - in about 15 mm sick lines under care of V.O. - Nos I, II, & III Sections marched to ST HILAIRE LILLERS. 1 pm - 2 pm & 3 pm respectively to ST HILAIRE, LILLERS. ALLOUAGNE & LOZENGHEM - 11 miles. All horses stabled in grounds of CHATEAU at LOZENGHEM.	J/F
27th March '15 LOZENGHEM	Four horses died - No IV Section arrived at 6 pm.	J/F
28 March '15	Under instructions from H.Q. 2nd LONDON DIV. the O/C Brigade proceeded to GONNEHEM to see the 2nd DIV AMN. COL. for instructions. - Three more horses died and a total of 35 in sick.	J/F
10 am. 29 March '15 LOZENGHEM	The G.O.C. 2nd LONDON DIV. inspected the Brigade and the reported the opinion that all harness, saddlery, riding clothing, horses much appeared fit for condition of the last fortnight since coming - More with horse lines on this respect - every defect and deep mud.	J/F

1247 W 8299 200,000 (E) 8/14 J.B.C. & A. Forms/C. 2118/11.

WAR DIARY
or
INTELLIGENCE SUMMARY
(Erase heading not required.)

Army Form C. 2118.

Instructions regarding War Diaries and Intelligence Summaries are contained in F. S. Regs., Part II. and the Staff Manual respectively. Title pages will be prepared in manuscript.

Hour, Date, Place	Summary of Events and Information	Remarks and references to Appendices
30 March '15. LOZENGHEM	5 Horses died one night - in spite of every care + attention - Anaemia. The more serious cases are not likely to recover - Fitting harness + cleaning under O/C Sections -	JW
31 March '15	do	JW
4.15pm 1st April '15	General MUNRO - G.O.C. 1st Army Corps. inspected the Column enroute LOZENGHEM-ALLOUAGNE Road + approved the general turn out. Short time to pass him on the country & the difficulties it had had to contend with "sore numbers" —	JW
2nd + 3rd April 15	All Sections engaged in arranging their interior economy. Drivers in harness + grooming. Repairing horses.	JW
4th April '15	3 horses died - Provisions Gazettes to date 19th March '15 LIEUT W SHELDON DICKASON to be CAPTAIN 2nd LIEUT J.C.D. KIMBER " LIEUT. " S. WHIGBORNE " " Weather very wet + inspection for sick horses - one more stable had been found for them so that they were taken back to be parked in the open under existence from A.D.V.S. 2nd Div.	JW
5th April '15	2 Remounts arrived from distribution 1 & 6 No 2 Section & 3 " N°.4 — 2 horses died.	JW
6th + 7th April '15	4 Wagons of Heavy (4.7in) Battery of N°4 Section under 2nd ALLCROFT opt to be attached to 1st DIVISION	JW One officer 2nd R.F. 16 A.D. 3 riders - head 4 Wagons + 1 G.S. wagon 2 horses + driver

WAR DIARY
or
INTELLIGENCE SUMMARY

(Erase heading not required.)

Army Form C. 2118.

Hour, Date, Place	Summary of Events and Information	Remarks and references to Appendices
7th April '15 LOZENGHEM	3 horses died. - All ranks receiving instruction in harnessing from Sergt. Major CLARKE attached temporarily from 5th LONDON BRIGADE R.F.A. T.F. O/C Column reports on writing to CAPT. BLACKBURN - ADJUTANT to Column - to BRIG. GEN. CECIL WRAY	
8th April '15	O/C Column proceeded to FOUQUEREUIL to inspect SECOND DIV. A.M.M. COL. - Sections carrying on their own work.	
9th April '15	O/C went with COLUMN INTERPRETER to FOUQUEREUIL and ANNEZIN to select picketing ground & huts for men in want of possible move & transport to C.R.A. 2nd LON DIV. MSTD Sections ammunition total 20 since 3rd April, including 4 machines, 2 rifles - no prisoners - no internal haemorrhage. Instructions issued to troops & transport, receiving from in	
10th AM 11th April '15 12th April '15	G.O.C. 2nd LONDON DIV. (General BARTER) inspected the Column at 12 noon & congratulated all ranks on the improvement of horses appearance. The O/C in the afternoon arranged to ANNEZIN - being sick horse in charge of Mobile Veterinary Section LOZENGHEM	
13th April '15 ANNEZIN 14th April '15	Instruction & detail in harnessing - care of harness - fitting of nosebags, mantica blankets etc, all of which were fully explained - N.C.O's formed into a class for the same purpose. Instruction given on chestiny [?]	

Army Form C. 2118.

WAR DIARY
or
INTELLIGENCE SUMMARY
(Erase heading not required.)

Instructions regarding War Diaries and Intelligence Summaries are contained in F. S. Regs., Part II. and the Staff Manual respectively. Title pages will be prepared in manuscript.

Hour, Date, Place	Summary of Events and Information	Remarks and references to Appendices
15th April 1915. ANNEZIN.	Brig. Genl. Cecil Wray C.R.A. 2nd London Divn. arrived Hinges about Horse Lines Wagon line. The Howitzer portion of No. 4 Section received orders at 3.30 p.m. to march early tomorrow for BELLERIVE. Capt. SHELDON DICKASON was sent in to arrange billets yesterday	Missing not state 1 Officer 57 R.F.? __52__ Horses H.D. 54 Riders 5 __52__
16th April	Howitzer portion of No. 4 Section marched off at 7.30 a.m. for BELLERIVE to take the attack to 7th Divn. Amm. Col. Officer, 20 other ranks left at 6.15 a.m. for CHOCQUES and brought back 18 L.D. amounts of single mounts. Capt. BLACKBURN - Adjutant to the Column - left without medical charge for 5th LONDON FIELD AMBULANCE	16 Amm. wagons 1 G.S. wagon 2 horses 1 driver ALLOWANCE
17th April	A Board of Survey on articles of clothing suitable for return to ORDNANCE Stores time held at 15th LONDON BRIGADE R.F.A. (T.F.) 1st LONDON BRIGADE (How.) PRESIDENT Lt. Col. A.C. LOWE D.S.O. Member Capt. G. EGERTON WARBURTON & Capt. A.D. WINK. The O/C went over to BELLERIVE to inspect No. 4 Section.	
18th April	Board of Survey continued at 6th LONDON BGDE - GORRE & 1st LONDON Bgde. LA BASSÉE Rd.	
19th April	2 H.D. remounts received from 5th LONDON Brigade Amm. Col. & transfer to No. 3 Section. 3 Rear Details arrived posted 1/6 No. 3 - Lt. Nott. O/C wrote pressing for medicine which have been frequently promised. At rear particularly - a number of men off duty from sickness which ought to avoid if proper medicine available.	
20th April	Instruction by O/C of Column known in writing order. Received memo that the 2nd LONDON DIVISION is henceforth called the LONDON DIVN.	

Army Form C. 2118.

WAR DIARY
or
INTELLIGENCE SUMMARY

(Erase heading not required.)

Instructions regarding War Diaries and Intelligence Summaries are contained in F. S. Regs., Part II. and the Staff Manual respectively. Title pages will be prepared in manuscript.

Hour, Date, Place	Summary of Events and Information	Remarks and references to Appendices
21st April 1915. ANNEZIN	The O/C inspected harness in skeleton order of No IV Section at BELLERIVE at 10 a.m. - Inspection of uniforms of Nos 1, 2 & 3 Sections at 2.30 p.m. 2nd Lieut F.T. CLARKE R.F.A. arrived & took up the duties of ADJUTANT to the Column	
22nd April 1915.	O/C visited 6th & 7th Bde A.M.M. Co's S. 1 horse returned from MOBILE VET. SECTION - LOZENGHIEM. Kits bags fetched from CHATEAU LOZENGHIEM.	
23rd April 1915.	1 horse (No 274) of No III Section, died of heart failure. Met inspection under Adjutant. Each section engaged in forwarding ammunition required by respective Bde Ammn Columns.	
24th April	O/C proceeded to NEUVILLE CHAPELLE to endeavour to find heavy portion of No II Section but found it had moved some distance north with the LAHORE DIV.	
25th	O/C inspected No IV Section at BELLERIVE. Two horses returned to No IV O: & No III Section from LOZENGHIEM. One horse - No II Section - destroyed by V.O.	
26th & 27th	1 Man - Gr PRITCHARD returned from hospital to No IV Sect (Heavy Portion) Parade in marching order - Sections supplying ammunition. Received news that will have to be & hand gunners are to be supplied thro' A.C.R.E. (not through A.M.M. Col's S.	

Army Form C. 2118.

WAR DIARY
or
INTELLIGENCE SUMMARY

(Erase heading not required.)

Instructions regarding War Diaries and Intelligence Summaries are contained in F. S. Regs., Part II. and the Staff Manual respectively. Title pages will be prepared in manuscript.

Hour, Date, Place	Summary of Events and Information	Remarks and references to Appendices
28th April 1915 ANNEZIN	The Column was inspected by G.O.C. LONDON DIV. in grounds of JARDIN DE SPORTS at 10 a.m. Extract from COLUMN ORDERS:— "The G.O.C. LONDON DIV. inspected the O/C Column to convey to all ranks how highly pleased he was with the appearance of the Column on parade this morning, taking into consideration the great improvement shown since the Column has been in this country."	M
29 April	Inspection for 2 Field Forges, no smith number of different items on the Column it is almost impossible to extemporise any more horses continuously.— One horse No 7 Section sick—	M
30 April	28 L.D. & 2 Riders marched from Renents from posts as follows L.D. H.S. 2, No.I 9, No.II 6, No.III 5, N° III 6. Riders No II 1, No III 1. The L.D. horses were of good class & the best draft of remounts yet supplied to the Column in France— Officers Riders practice.	M

1247 W 3299 200,000 (E) 8/14 J.B.C. & A. Forms/C. 2118/11.

121/5482

47th Div Amm Col
Vol II 1 — 30. 5. 15

Army Form C. 2118.

WAR DIARY
or
INTELLIGENCE SUMMARY
(Erase heading not required.)

LONDON DIV. AMM. COL.

Hour, Date, Place	Summary of Events and Information	Remarks and references to Appendices
1st May 1915 ANNEZIN.	LON. DIV. AMM. PARK notified they had no further 15 pr. ammunition in hand for issue. - I indented for the same 560 rounds 95 m.m. Trench mortar ammunition. Owing to many indents coming in from Infantry Brigades in an irregular manner - request was made to Divisional HQs that Infantry Brigades should be reminded to indent for S.A.A. ammunition in accordance with Field Service Regulations Part I paras 158, 159, 160.	
2nd May 1915.	Urgent indent for trench mortar ammunition received from O/C 1st Bat. LONDON REGT. H.R. RUE DE L'EPINETTE. O/C Column furnished the information but notified 21st that personally that no further requisitions would be fulfilled except through BDE AMM COLS. Board of Survey called to report on homings, horse blankets, and great coats to be returned to RAILHEAD.	
3rd May 1915.	Report was made that the D.A.C. should carry 35 rounds complete per trench mortar round in the Division. This would necessitate carrying less black gunpowder used for charges. The O/C represented this would be considerable danger to the rest of the ammunition if this had to be carried out. On enquiry from the 1st and 2nd DIV. AMM COLS ascertained that they were not allowed to carry such ammunition but only to indent for it as required.	

1247 W 8290 200,000 (E) 8/14 J.B.C. & A. Forms/C. 2118/11.

Army Form C. 2118.

WAR DIARY
or
INTELLIGENCE SUMMARY
(Erase heading not required.)

LONDON D.A.C.

Instructions regarding War Diaries and Intelligence Summaries are contained in F. S. Regs., Part II. and the Staff Manual respectively. Title pages will be prepared in manuscript.

Hour, Date, Place	Summary of Events and Information	Remarks and references to Appendices
4th May 1915 ANNEZIN	O/C Column visited No. IV Section at BELLERIVE. Horses and harness well cared for. O/C No. IV Section reported having found a considerable quantity of Government stores in an Estaminet near the line - the stores were properties + a list of them forwarded to A.P.M. 2nd Division. All billets were visited - found clean + in good order.	N/L
5th May '15.	No. IV Section moved to CORNET MALO - attached to 1st Div. Amm. Col. - O/C Column inspected Section before marching off. Orders received from Divl. H.Q. that black powder to not to be carried by the Column on account of danger by explosion. Dr. Spencer No. I Section returned from 5th Lon. FIELD AMBc.	No. IV Section marching off state 1 Officer 53 Other ranks 16 Hor. Am. wagons 66 H.D.+L.D. horses 5 Riders. N/L
6th May '15	Issued 600 rounds 15 pr. ammn: extra per 5th, 6th + 7th. London Brigades R.F.A. = 50 rounds per gun - also 20 rounds per gun 5" Howitzer Bgde. = 206 rounds. O/C went to No. IV Section at CORNET MALO.	N/L
7th May '15	Issued 1,200,000 rounds S.A.A. - 80 Hales Rifle Grenades d/100 the black powder for trench mortars to 5th + 6th London Inf. Bdes. All horses in Column showing considerable improvement owing to getting in better condition + favourable weather.	N/L

Army Form C. 2118.

WAR DIARY
or
INTELLIGENCE SUMMARY
(Erase heading not required.)

47th (Lon) DIV. AMM. COL.

Hour, Date, Place	Summary of Events and Information	Remarks and references to Appendices
8th May 1915 ANNEZIN	Paraded in marching order same returns fact. — General engagement by 1st & 2nd Div's & LONDON DIV'N. — Expended units of 6th inst. — Ammunition granted is 15 pm + S.A. Ammunition forwarded to 5th 6th & 7th R.F.A. Bde Amm. Col's and drawn from AMM. PARK to fill up	HH
9th May 1915	Paraded marching order 5 am. Artillery gone fire 4.45 am. Infantry assault 5.40. – Artillery again in fire at 3.20 pm. " " 4 pm – Both reserved orders to beat things to enemy's lines.	HH
10th May '15	14 L.D. Remounts arrived two's posted as per margin. — These complete the number of horses of establishment. — Also bought from CHOCQUES Station 15 horses for 5th 6th & 7th R.F.A. Bde's R.F.A. & 1 for 8th How BDE all of which were handed over.	H.Q. 1 No I Section 3 " II " 4 " III " 3 " IV " 3 HH
11th May '15	Inspection of Sections in marching order inspected. 1 horse destroyed by V.O. (broken leg)	HH
12th May '15	Future designation of the Div'n is to be 47th (London) DIVISION in place of 2/2nd London Div'n. (Authority War Office letter 47/W.O./2481 (A.G.1) dated 7th May 1915. – Future address of D.A.C. to be 47th D.A.C.	HH

Army Form C. 2118.

WAR DIARY
or
INTELLIGENCE SUMMARY 47th (Ln) DIV. AMN. COL.
(Erase heading not required.)

Instructions regarding War Diaries and Intelligence Summaries are contained in F. S. Regs., Part II. and the Staff Manual respectively. Title pages will be prepared in manuscript.

Hour, Date, Place	Summary of Events and Information	Remarks and references to Appendices
ANNEZIN 15th May 1915	O/C Column received orders from G.O.C. R.A. to proceed at once to 6th Lon Bde FA and assume Command. Leaving in compliance at 11.45 A.M.	
18th May 1915	In accordance with 47th Lon Div Art orders issued on the night of 17th, Major R.R. Wansbrough, 6th Lond. B.A.C. assumed and took Command. One Officer and 7 men from Base reported as reinforcement, were detailed and proceeded	
19th 20th 21st May 1915	Inspection of Nos 1, 2 and 3 Sections upon taking over. During these days an intermittent bombardment commenced; shells falling within 150 yards of our position. The enemy usually firing between 7.30 and 6.30 A.M and 4.30 and 5.30 P.M. By order of Div Art two Billoting parties sent to shed FONTNELLE FARMS for 5th Lon FA.	

Army Form C. 2118.

WAR DIARY
or
INTELLIGENCE SUMMARY
(Erase heading not required.)

47th LON. DIV. AM:IN COL

Hour, Date, Place	Summary of Events and Information	Remarks and references to Appendices
AHNEZIN 23 May 1915 4.0 PM	case Emergency more desirable. Later in day harassed up and about by. When bombardment again commenced and became again more dangerous, moved E.8.d.3.4. near	
FOUQUEREUIL 6.30 PM	t:- map 1/10000. FOUQUEREUIL arriving at 6.30. went into Bivouac. In accordance with H.Q. Div Arty orders supplied 19th Battery 6th LON. F.A. with 1000 15 pr "HADFIELD" Shrapnel and received unexpended ammunition 1 allotted to Max Brigade Capt A Hurt ordered to join Col.	DNN
11 AM FOUQUEREUIL 24/27 May 1915	Delivery Ammunition to BAC.s Parking Vehicles Rearranging Horse lines and Bivouac. Inspecting full Harness and Equipment. Rifles &c	

1247 W 3299 200,000 (E) 8/14 J.B.C. & A. Forms/C. 2118/11.

Army Form C. 2118.

WAR DIARY
~~INTELLIGENCE SUMMARY~~ 47th LON. DIV AMM. COL

(Erase heading not required.)

Instructions regarding War Diaries and Intelligence Summaries are contained in F.S. Regs., Part II. and the Staff Manual respectively. Title pages will be prepared in manuscript.

Hour, Date, Place	Summary of Events and Information	Remarks and references to Appendices
FOUGUEREUIL May 24/27	Unable to supply incidents for HALE Rifle Grenades. AMMN PARK also unable to supply for many days. No. 1 Section 2nd D.A.C. arrived and reported.	
May 28/30	No 4 Section Hawkins rejoined. Lieut B.S. Netherton posted to 5th Lon. Brigade F.A. and proceeded. 2/Lieut A. Keir arrived in everyway.	

Army Form C. 2118.

WAR DIARY
or
INTELLIGENCE SUMMARY

(*Erase heading not required.*)

Instructions regarding War Diaries and Intelligence Summaries are contained in F. S. Regs., Part II. and the Staff Manual respectively. Title pages will be prepared in manuscript.

Hour, Date, Place	Summary of Events and Information	Remarks and references to Appendices

1247 W 3259 200,000 (E) 8/14 J.B.C.&A. Forms/C. 2118/1.

Army Form C. 2118.

WAR DIARY
or
INTELLIGENCE SUMMARY   49yn (Lon) Div. A.M.M. CCC.
(Erase heading not required.)

Instructions regarding War Diaries and Intelligence Summaries are contained in F. S. Regs., Part II. and the Staff Manual respectively. Title pages will be prepared in manuscript.

Hour, Date, Place	Summary of Events and Information	Remarks and references to Appendices
ANNEZIN 22 May 1915	In accordance with Div Art orders supplied 6th Lon Fty with full complement of new 80 fuzed 15 Pdr Ammunition for 2 Batteries and B.A.C. complete. Receiving in exchange all old unexpended ammunition. The customary morning and afternoon bombardment continued. A correction apparently been made and shells heavy apparently been made and shells falling nearer our position. One on our sick lines and one close to No 3 section horse lines. Moved No 3 horse lines.	
23 May 1915 11 A.M.	Corrected. 22 Remounts from C H O Q U E S (?) order of Div Arty and disposed as instructed. Reported at Art H.Q. that the shelling might indicate registration upon our position, information as to no fall of the projectiles being easily obtainable by the enemy. Authorised to reconnoitre in	

101/599

47th Division

47th Div: Amm: Col"

Vol III 1 — 30.6.16.

a⁻
a16.

"A" Form. Army Form C. 2121.

MESSAGES AND SIGNALS.

Prefix Code m.	Words	Charge	This message is on a/c of:	Recd. at m.
Office of Origin and Service Instructions.	Sent			Date
	At m.		Service.	From
	To			
	By		(Signature of "Franking Officer")	By

TO Head Quarters
47th Divisional Artillery

Sender's Number	Day of Month	In reply to Number		AAA
RRW 154	Nil			

War Diary for past month sent this day

From D/C 47th Div Arty
Place
Time

The above may be forwarded as now corrected. (Z)

Censor. Signature of Addressor or person authorised to telegraph in his name
* This line should be erased if not required.

Army Form C. 2118.

WAR DIARY
or
INTELLIGENCE SUMMARY   4/4th (London) Div R.A.M.C

(Erase heading not required.)

Instructions regarding War Diaries and Intelligence Summaries are contained in F. S. Regs., Part II. and the Staff Manual respectively. Title pages will be prepared in manuscript.

Hour, Date, Place	Summary of Events and Information	Remarks and references to Appendices
1st June 1915 FOUQUEREUIL	Instructions from H.Q. Div Arty to reconnoitre for a position near VAUDRICOURT. Ref map BETHUNE 1/20,000 K4. Selected position K3 & 38 await orders so to move. AMM PARK again reported shortage of 4.5" H.E. Grenades esp. Jelly & Hy Smk. none available.	(over)
2nd June 1915 FOUQUEREUIL 9.30 A.M. VAUDRICOURT	Orders from H.Q. Div Arty to move near VAUDRICOURT and proceeded at 9.30 AM. Ref Map BETHUNE) K3. d.2.8. Queries about reinforcing the 6x LON TA. Sent up another 10 men. Reinforcements from Base very slow. 20 men have been sent for LON TA and none arrived from Base. Serious shortage. New 15 PDR 80 Fused Shrapnel coming very slowly. 200 Rds in 2 days only.	(over)
3rd June VAUDRICOURT	Ordered to find picketing and Bivouac for the 14th Battery 5"6 Lon Briged and arranged area adjoining our Unit. Again no 13 Pdr Am" from Park	(over)

1247 W 3299 200,000 (E) 8/14 J.B.C. & A. Forms/C. 2118/11.

Army Form C. 2118.

WAR DIARY
or
INTELLIGENCE SUMMARY

(Erase heading not required.)

47th DIV. ARMY. COL:

Instructions regarding War Diaries and Intelligence Summaries are contained in F. S. Regs., Part II. and the Staff Manual respectively. Title pages will be prepared in manuscript.

Hour, Date, Place	Summary of Events and Information	Remarks and references to Appendices
4th June VAUDRICOURT 5th June	This Unit visited by HRH Prince of Wales. 10th Bty 5th Lon Brigade marched in. Orders to find room for 18th Baty. 4th Lon Brigade and allotted area. Again no Amn at Park 7th 15 Pdr Batteries.	
6th June	18th Battery 4th Lon Brigade marched in. Received orders to issue new 15 Pdr 80 Anged Shrapnel to 19th Battery and issued 324 Rds receiving 320 Rds 15 Pr in exchange. Camp visited by Mr General Barter.	
7th June	Church Parade. Chaplain 4th Field Ambulance. 10th and 18th Batteries marched out. The Adjutant Captn L. J. Clarke RFA and Captn M. S. Duckison o/c Res Section proceeded on Leave. During absence of Adjutant deputed Captn Maybulin, acting 19th Battery. ordered to find area 7m Major Lens.	

1247 W 3290 200,000 (E) 8/14 J.B.C.&A. Forms/C. 2118/11.

WAR DIARY
or
INTELLIGENCE SUMMARY

(Erase heading not required.)

Army Form C. 2118.

4 Yr (L'pn) Div. Amm Col.

Hour, Date, Place	Summary of Events and Information	Remarks and references to Appendices
8th June 1915 VAUDRICOURT	Received orders that the Artillery of the Division was going into Reserve. Ordered to Reconnoitre for a Rot Bivouac in the neighbourhood of BOIS DES DAMES South of LAPUGNOY. Reconnoitred and reported. Killed my Charger Head apoplexy attempt. Test run back more than half way.	(M)
9th June VAUDRICOURT 6 a.m. BOIS DES DAMES	Applied once again for facilities for Motor travel. Third application. Ordered to move to D29 d. Ref Map BETHUNE 1/40000. Marched out and arrived BOIS DES DAMES 6 a.m. Issuing of S.A.A. part of Column and 4 Maxim Gun Section No 3. with new 80 Fuze Shrapnel at VAUDRICOURT under Capth Warburton.	(N)
10/14th June BOIS DES DAMES	In Reserve, A.M.M. PARK commenced delivering 15 Pdr Shrapnel on 14th when 1000 Rounds issued. Bosin Mot/Ro Date 11.6.'15. Detached Section at AROUVIN issuing a little S.A.A. re. ART. Brigades in Reserve.	(O)

1247 W 3299 200,000 (E) 8/14 J.B.C. & A. Forms/C.2118/11.

Army Form C. 2118.

WAR DIARY
or
INTELLIGENCE SUMMARY
(Erase heading not required.)

47th (LON) Div. Amm. Col.

Instructions regarding War Diaries and Intelligence Summaries are contained in F. S. Regs., Part II. and the Staff Manual respectively. Title pages will be prepared in manuscript.

Hour, Date, Place	Summary of Events and Information	Remarks and references to Appendices
June 15/30 BOIS DES DAMES	In Reserve. By this date (30.6.15) the unit had been supplied with 15 Pdr Ammn up to Establishment. The F.A. Brigades are still about 3000 Rounds short. This is however partially due to the possession of changing from 63 and 65 Fuzes Shell to the new 80 Fuze.	[signature] R.W.... Major Commanding 47th (Lon) Div A.C.

"A" Form.   Army Form C. 2121.
MESSAGES AND SIGNALS.

TO: 47 DAC

Sender's Number: BM 214   Day of Month: 4   AAA

Please forward DIARY direct to Base as per Divisional Artillery Routine Order No. 148 dated 3rd June 1915

From: 47 DIV ARTY

Time: 7.25 pm

121/6410

47th Division

47 th Divl. Ammn Coln

Vol IV

From 1st to 31st July 1915.

Army Form C. 2118.

WAR DIARY
or
INTELLIGENCE SUMMARY   47th DIV. AMM. COL.

(Erase heading not required.)

Instructions regarding War Diaries and Intelligence Summaries are contained in F. S. Regs, Part II. and the Staff Manual respectively. Title pages will be prepared in manuscript.

Hour, Date, Place	Summary of Events and Information	Remarks and references to Appendices
July 1 – 31 BOIS DES DAMES	Remained in Bivouac here. The Division being in Reserve to a great extent. The Brigades R.F.A. consisted most of the month. Arrangements being completed for the employment of the Wagons & teams of this Unit in the work of conveying Material to the R.E. in the front line. When not so engaged making every effort to keep the Unit up to a high state of efficiency by frequent Inspections. Route marches and so on.	A.V.D.B. R.R. Wemdrypan Comm. 7th Div. Am. Col.

121/
17599

47th Division

47th Div Ammn. Col.

Aug - Sep 1915

Vol I

Army Form C. 2118.

WAR DIARY
or
INTELLIGENCE SUMMARY   47th London Divisional Ammunition Column

(Erase heading not required.)

Hour, Date, Place	Summary of Events and Information	Remarks and references to Appendices
1915 Aug 11 Bois des Dames D.2.6.d.1.6.	Capt. E. C. White of 8th London Brigade R.F.A. having taken command of No 4 Section is taken on strength	
Aug 16	Major R.R. Woodbridge, relinquishes the command of the 47th Div. Ammunition Column. Major H.G. McLea, from 7th London Brigade R.F.A. (18th London Battery) took over the command	
Aug 19	Lt H.C.D Kimber attached to 7th London Brigade R.F.A.	
	During the month of August the unit besides supplying ammunition to Brigades carried out cutting work for the R.E.	

H.G. McLea
Major
O/C 47 L.D.A.C.

Army Form C. 2118.

Page 1

WAR DIARY
or
INTELLIGENCE SUMMARY 47th London Divisional Ammunition Column
(Erase heading not required.)

Hour, Date, Place	Summary of Events and Information	Remarks and references to Appendices
1915 Sept 2 Bois des Dames	One section of 1st Divisional Ammunition Column under Major Thompson attached to this Column and moved into bivouac at LABUISSIERE J.5.c.3.8.	
Sept 5 LABUISSIERE Sept 18	The Column moved to LABUISSIERE and bivouaced at J.5.c.5.5. In accordance with orders 36 G.S. wagons had been received as silent on the road as possible. Wheels had straw packed on the tyres secured with cord and old motor car tyres secured over the straw packing. Seats and brakes were removed and all loose articles secured to be free from rattle. Leather shoes were made for the fore feet of wheel horses. The wagons under the command of Major 14th Head Capts C Egerton Warburton and Capt A A Brink proceeded to Forse 8 VERQUIN E 30.c.2.2. arriving at 6 pm. The	

WAR DIARY

INTELLIGENCE SUMMARY

Army Form C. 2118.

Page 2

47th Div. Ammun. Column

Hour, Date, Place	Summary of Events and Information	Remarks and references to Appendices
1915 Sept. 18 LABUISSIERE	Wagons were there loaded up with gas cylinders. Each cylinder, in a box, 14 in. each wagon, and in parties of six wagons the whole moved via NOEUX LES MINES and MAZINGARBE and LES BREBIS to GRENAY M.2.b.7.5. where the wagons were unloaded by parties of infantry between 10 p.m. and midnight, the cylinders being carried into the trenches and the boxes being returned by the wagons to FOSSE 8. From that place the wagons proceeded to the DISTILLERIE, NOEUX LES MINES K.24.a 6.9. arriving at 4.30 a.m. on the 19th. and bivouacked.	
Sept 1. 19	The wagons as the DISTILLERIE. NOEUX LES MINES. carried out similar work to that done the previous night. The unloading at LABUISSIERE by 5 a.m. on 20th Sept. the wagons was successful but the leather shoes for the horses were found unwearable. The material available not being substantial enough for the heavy use. The work on	

WAR DIARY or INTELLIGENCE SUMMARY

Page 3 Army Form C. 2118.

47th Div. Ammunition Column

Hour, Date, Place	Summary of Events and Information	Remarks and references to Appendices
LA BUSSIERE 1915 Sep 22	Both nights were not interrupted by shell fire. Six wagons with from three teams from 5th, 6th & 7th London Brigades R.F.A. joined in attachment to Column (18 wagons & 72 horses in all). One section of 20th Div. Ammunition Column attached and bivouaced at LA BUSSIERE	
26	Section of 24th D.A.C. left to rejoin their unit at BEUVRY at 11 A.M. 2nd Lt Davies having left the unit to take charge of 47th Div. Ammunition Dump at MAZINGARBE on 23rd Sept reported	
27	The section of 1st Divisional Ammunition Column left to rejoin their unit. The Column is in addition to supplying ammunition carried out cartridge work for the R.E. during the month of September.	

H Gohen Major
O/C 47th D.A.C.

Army Form C. 2118.

47th Div Ammunition Column

WAR DIARY
or
INTELLIGENCE SUMMARY
(Erase heading not required.)

Instructions regarding War Diaries and Intelligence Summaries are contained in F. S. Regs., Part II. and the Staff Manual respectively. Title pages will be prepared in manuscript.

Hour, Date, Place	Summary of Events and Information	Remarks and references to Appendices
1915 Oct 7 LABUSSIERE	Twelve g.s. waggons and teams on carting work for R.E. Five horses killed six wounded and one waggon destroyed by shell fire at LE RUTOIRE near VERMELLES G.15.6.	
Oct 25	Weather cold and unsettled, billets found for all men	
28	Capt and Adjutant J. J. Clarke R.F.A. to 47th Divisional Artillery Headquarters for duty temporarily	
29	39 g.s. waggons and 156 heavy draught horses (including those attached) proceeded to transport depot ABBEVILLE under 2nd in L. division	

H. G. Menn
Major
O/c 47th D.A.C.

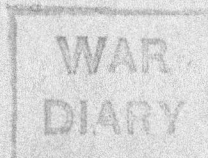

DIVISIONAL AMMUNITION COLUMN.

(47th Division)

S E P T E M B E R

1 9 1 5

Army Form C. 2118.

WAR DIARY
or
INTELLIGENCE SUMMARY

(Erase heading not required.)

Vol 14.

Instructions regarding War Diaries and Intelligence Summaries are contained in F.S. Regs., Part II. and the Staff Manual respectively. Title pages will be prepared in manuscript.

Hour, Date, Place	Summary of Events and Information	Remarks and references to Appendices
HALLICOURT 1/9/15	Lieut. Col. Capt. LAPUGNOY at 2.30 pm for HALLICOURT travelling via BRUAY. Lieut Lorimer returned from 73rd Bde. R.F.A. Field Officer on Divisional Communication.	
HALLICOURT 2-3/9/15	Making Presence.	do
HALLICOURT 4/9/15	24 Rounds returned 10 P.dr Battery. 192 complete rounds issued to 12 m Battery.	do
HALLICOURT 5/9/15	Capt. Gwinn attached to 5th Battery. Marking Presence.	do
HALLICOURT 6/9/15	368 rounds 5 P.dr Ammunition returned to D.A.C. 365 rounds 4065 Ammunition on return.	do
	50 rounds 40 P.dr 22 m Battery firing line. 50 rds 50 lbs on return.	do
HALLICOURT 7/9/15	318 rds 5 P.dr returned to D.A.C. 1 G.S. wagon returned by 22 m Battery.	do
HALLICOURT 8/9/15	96 Rounds 40 lbs Ammunition taken to 22 m Battery wagon line - 96 Rounds 50 lbs	do
	Ammunition 5 P.dr. Ammunition returned to D.A.C. 40 Rounds 40 lbs Ammunition reserve	
	received from D.A.C.	
	96 Rounds 5 P.dr Ammunition returned to 5-DAC. 144 Rounds 40 lbs Ammunition reserve	
	90 Rounds 40 lbs Ammunition issued to 22 m Battery wagon line - 90 Rounds 50 lbs	
	Ammunition returned to D.A.C.	
	80 Rounds 40 lbs Ammunition issued to 12 m Battery wagon line - 90 Rounds 50 lbs	
	Ammunition returned to D.A.C.	
HALLICOURT 9/9/15	Marking Presence continues.	
HALLICOURT 11/9/15	Marking Interview. Capt. Gwinn returned to A. Col. from 51st Battery	do
HALLICOURT 12/9/15	68 Rounds 40 lbs Ammunition issued to 22 m Battery wagon line.	do
	259 Rounds 5 P.dr Ammunition and 281 Rounds 40 lbs Ammunition reserve	
	from D.A.C.	
	145 Rounds 40 lbs Ammunition issued to 21 st Battery wagon line	
	446 " " " " "	
HALLICOURT 13/9/15	Marking Presence	do
HALLICOURT 14/9/15	160 Rounds 5 P.dr Ammunition issued to 22 m Battery W.L. 48 Rounds	do
	40 lbs Ammunition returned from 22 m Batt. W.L. to Am. Col.	
	440 Rounds 40 lbs returned to D.A.P.	

Army Form C. 2118.

WAR DIARY
or
INTELLIGENCE SUMMARY.
(Erase heading not required.)

Vol. 15

Instructions regarding War Diaries and Intelligence Summaries are contained in F.S. Regs., Part II. and the Staff Manual respectively. Title pages will be prepared in manuscript.

Place	Date	Hour	Summary of Events and Information	Remarks and references to Appendices
HALLICOURT	14/9/15		159 Rounds 50cb Ammunition received from D.A.C. 85 Rounds 40cb returned to D.A.C. 27 Rounds 40cb issued to 21st Bde. W.L. 74 Rounds 40cb returned to Am. Col. from 22nd Battery W.L.	
HALLICOURT	16/9/15		49 Rounds 50cb issued to 22nd Battery W.L. Watching Exercise for all horses. 209 Rounds 50cb and 12 rounds 40cb issued to 21st Battery W.L. Watching Exercise continues.	
HALLICOURT	17/9/15		249 Rounds 40cb received from D.A.C. and 250 rounds 40cb issued to 22nd Battery W.L. 100 T. issued to 21st Battery wagon line. Watching Exercise.	
HALLICOURT	18/9/15	9am	Watching Exercise.	
HALLICOURT	19/9/15		193 Rounds 40cb received from D.A.C. 169 Rounds 40cb issued to 21st Battery W.L.	
		9am	Watching Exercise.	
		9..	Watching Exercise.	
HALLICOURT	20/9/15	2.30pm to 4.30pm	Instruction in Signalling for 3 men and Telephony for 9 men. 53 Rounds 40cb received from D.A.C. 57 Rounds 40cb issued to 21st Battery W.L.	
HALLICOURT	21/9/15	9am	Watching Exercise.	
		2.30 to 4.30pm	Signalling and Telephone instruction for 3 & 9 men respectively.	
		11pm	600 Rounds 40cb received from D.A.C. and 500 Rounds 40cb issued to 21st Battery Wagon Line.	
			196 Rounds 40cb issued to 22nd Battery Wagon Line	

1577 Wt. W10791/1773 500,000 1/15 D.D.&L. A.D.S.S./Forms/C. 2118.

WAR DIARY
or
INTELLIGENCE SUMMARY.
(Erase heading not required.)

Army Form C. 2118.

Vol. 16

Place	Date	Hour	Summary of Events and Information	Remarks and references to Appendices
HAILLICOURT	22/9/15	9 am 4.30 pm 4.30-7.30 pm	Washing Exercise. 237 Tubes, 479 Rings, 428 Caps, 74 Rings 428 Caps, 455 Cent Covers reed to D.A.C Signalling & Telephone instruction. Ammunition for 12 mm 4th Rounds 40 lb received from D.A.C. 288 Reed 40 lb issued to 22nd Battery Wagon lines. 30 T Tubes issued to 21st Battery W.R. 34 Rounds 40 lb received from D.A.C. ammunition from 22nd Battery Wagon lines off.	
HAILLICOURT	23/9/15	2.30 pm-5 5.30 pm 3.30 pm-10.30 pm	Washing Exercise. 278 Tubes, 288 Rings, 282 Caps, 591 Rings, 248 Cent Covers reed to D.A.C Signalling and Telephone instruction for 12 mm 124 Rounds 40 lb received from D.A.C. Washing Service.	
HAILLICOURT	24/9/15	10.30 am	Signalling and telephone for 12 mm 136 Rounds 40 lb issued to 21 at Battery W.R.	
HAILLICOURT	25/9/15	9 am	Washing Exercise. 500 Rounds 40 lb received from D.A.C. 252 Rounds 40 lb issued to 21st Batt W.R. 248 Rounds 40 lb issued to 22nd Batt. W.R. 1794 Tubes (approx), 37 Tubes (impound), 1591 Rings, 1567 Caps, 1101 Rings, 1361 Cent Covers reed to D.A.C.	
HAILLICOURT	26/9/15	9 am	Washing Exercise. 2 mm attached to 21st Battery at NOEUX-LES-MINES for signalling instruction. 204 Rounds 40 lb received from D.A.C. 122 Rounds 40 lb issued to 21st Batt. W.R. and 80 Rounds 40 lb issued to 22nd Batt W.R. 70 Rounds 50 lb received from D.A.C.	
HAILLICOURT	27/9/15	9 am	Washing Exercise. 648 Rounds 40 lb received from D.A.C. and 648 Rounds 40 lb issued to 22 mm Battery 230 Rounds 50 lb received from D.A.C and 230 Rounds 50 lb issued to D.A.C. 22 nd 148 Rounds 40 lb received from D.A.C. 89 Rounds 40 lb issued to 21st Batt W.R and 59 Rounds 40 lb issued to 22 mm Battery W.R.	
HAILLICOURT	28/9/15	9 am	Washing Exercise. 675 Rounds 50 lb received from D.A.C. 382 Rounds 50 lb issued to 21st Batt. W.R and 291 Rounds 50 lb issued to 22nd Batt. W.R.	
HAILLICOURT	29/9/15	9 am	Washing Exercise. 1 No. James Tn D.019 arrived at	
HAILLICOURT	30/9/15	9 am	Washing Service.	

Army Form C. 2118.

WAR DIARY
or
INTELLIGENCE SUMMARY.
(Erase heading not required.)

Vol. 17

Place	Date	Hour	Summary of Events and Information	Remarks and references to Appendices
			Ammunition for the month	
			50th	
			Reserve and issues to Batteries 1585	
			Received from Batteries and returned to D.A.C. 1410	
			40th	
			Receive from D.A.C. 4720	
			Issued to Batteries 4914	
			Reserves from Batteries 522	
			Returned to D.A.C. 325	
			Totals Issues to Date. 4193*	
			40th.	
			50 lb	
			*4137 + 175 = 4312	
			*Issued to and of August, and including 400 Rounds returned to D.A.C. in exchange for H.E. shell.	
			[signature] Capt.	

Ammn. Col. 47th Dn.

Nov.

Vol. VI

121
7722

Army Form C. 2113.

Page 1

WAR DIARY
INTELLIGENCE SUMMARY

47th Div. Ammunition Column

(Erase heading not required.)

Hour, Date, Place	Summary of Events and Information	Remarks and references to Appendices
1915 Nov. 1 LABUISSIERE Nov 3	2/Lt HAMILTON DAVIES transferred to 6th Howitzer F.A.B.	
5	Lt.H.C.D. KIMBER transferred to 7th Howitzer F.A.B. Capt. C. EGERTON-WARBURTON left on attachment to 4th BATTERY R.F.A.	
14	Orders received from Divisional Artillery that unit would be equipped under Mobilization Store Table AFG 1098 - 181 The number of wagons thus being increased to a total of 86 in the four sections unit.	
16	Leaves of No light strength horses No 1 Section attached to 1st Div. Ammn Column to supply 5th LONDON F.A.B. in action. 147th that Divisional ammunition park building. No 1 Section made up to 1728 rounds	
AUCHEL 17	Column ordered to AUCHEL and went to MAZINGARBE	
18	billets (less No 1 Section). Horse lines at C 21 Nos 2 & 3 Sections made up to 3024 rounds of 18 pr ammunition	
20	School of instruction for junior Officers and NCOs from 5th, 6th, 7th and 8th LONDON F.A. BRIGADES. Nine Officers and 24 NCOs join for instruction	

Army Form C. 2118.

Page 2

WAR DIARY
INTELLIGENCE SUMMARY — 47th DIV. AMMUNITION COLUMN

(Erase heading not required.)

Hour, Date, Place	Summary of Events and Information	Remarks and references to Appendices
AUCHEL 1915 Nov 23	HARDING Lt. R. Harding of 8th LONDON. T.F.A.B. joined on attachment for duty	
29	CAPT. C.W. EGERTON WARBURTON rejoined from attachment to 4.6th BATTERY R.F.A. School of Instruction dispersed in accordance with orders received from G.O.C. R.A.	

H.G. Mead
Major
O/c. 47th DIV. AMMUN.
COLUMN.

47jii Dr Annu S. Co.

Dani

Vol VII

… Page 1 Army Form C. 2118.

WAR DIARY
INTELLIGENCE SUMMARY
47. Divisional Ammunition Column

(Erase heading not required.)

Instructions regarding War Diaries and Intelligence Summaries are contained in F.S. Regs., Part II. and the Staff Manual respectively. Title pages will be prepared in manuscript.

Hour, Date, Place	Summary of Events and Information	Remarks and references to Appendices
1915 Dec 1 AUCHEL	at 9.30 am AUCHEL. The Unit marched from AUCHEL in accordance with Divisional Orders for route march to starting point Cross Roads 600 yds West of first B of BURBURE and via ECQUEDECQUE – BOURECQ – ST HILAIRE – ROMBLY to Crossroads at first M of MAZINGHEM and then West to LIETTRES arriving at 4 pm and went into billets	MAP HAZEBROUCK 1/100,000
LIETTRES Dec 2	The Unit marched at 11 am to starting point, Crossroads North of third E in ESTRÉE BLANCHE and via TERFAY to AUCHEL returning to billets previously occupied at 4 pm	
3	The three lines being in a very bad state owing to the soft ground and bad weather arrangements were made with TOWN COMMANDANT to move lines and occupy billets on S.E. side of AUCHEL in Corons at C 28 d.	

1247 W 3299 200,000 (E) 8/14 J.B.C. & A. Forms/C. 2118/11.

WAR DIARY

INTELLIGENCE SUMMARY — 47th DIVISIONAL AMMUNITION COLUMN

Army Form C. 2118. Page 2

Hour, Date, Place	Summary of Events and Information	Remarks and references to Appendices
AUCHEL 1915 Sept 4	CAPT. L.C. BARRY and No 1 Section (less 2Lt VICK and 4 wagons and teams) rejoined from 1st D.A.C. School of Instruction again formed — 10 Officers and 24 NCOs from 5th 6th (7th and) 8th LONDON F.A. BDES.	
13	School of Instruction dispersed as 47th DIVISION was about to move up into action	
5	2Lt O'MALLEY transferred to this unit from 6th LONDON F.A.B. and posted to No 2 Section	
14	LT. BLAKE joined unit from ENGLAND and posted to No 1 Section	
GOSNAY 16	In accordance with orders the Column marched out of AUCHEL and went into billets at GOSNAY. No 3 Section 15th D.A.C. attached to supply 72nd and 73rd BDES R.F.A. 2LT VICK and 4 wagons	

Army Form C. 2118.

Page 3   47th DIVISIONAL AMMUNITION COLUMN

WAR DIARY
or
INTELLIGENCE SUMMARY
(Erase heading not required.)

Hour, Date, Place	Summary of Events and Information	Remarks and references to Appendices
GOSNAY Dec 16 1915	and teams rejoined from 1st D.A.C.	
18	Orders received from 47th Div. to move into lines lately occupied by 15th D.A.C. at HESDIGNEUL. Inspection of those lines showed that for the most part they were from 6 to 18 inches under liquid mud and heaps of rotting manure. Report was forwarded to 47th DIV. ARTILLERY	
HESDIGNEUL 19	The Unit moved to HESDIGNEUL as ordered	
20	Horses and lines inspected by DDR and BDR GENERAL WRAY	
23	150 mules and 52 H.D. horses taken over at NOEUX LES MINES and taken on strength	
25	40 H.D horses received and taken on strength. The Unit being 100 men below Establishment	

Page 4

Army Form C. 2118.

WAR DIARY
or
INTELLIGENCE SUMMARY

47th DIV. AMMUNITION COLUMN

(Erase heading not required.)

Hour, Date, Place	Summary of Events and Information	Remarks and references to Appendices
1915 Dec 25 HESDIGNEUL	and because of the large number of remounts received the difficulty of looking after the animals and training the drivers in addition to the usual work of supplying ammunition became very heavy. The attention of 47th Div. ARTILLERY was drawn to this position. H.G. Mead Major O/c 47th D.A.C.	

47th Sind Ormne'r. Col.

Jan

Vol VIII

Army Form C. 2118.

47 I. Div. Ammunition Column

WAR DIARY
INTELLIGENCE SUMMARY
(Erase heading not required.)

Instructions regarding War Diaries and Intelligence Summaries are contained in F. S. Regs., Part II. and the Staff Manual respectively. Title pages will be prepared in manuscript.

Hour, Date, Place	Summary of Events and Information	Remarks and references to Appendices
19/6 Jan 1 HESDIGNEUL	Orders received from 47th Div. to indent on SUB PARK for 45 box Mills Grenades 75000 S.A.A. and other ammunition which would be presently required.	
Jan 3/4	36 G.S. wagons with grenades, S.A.A. & other ammunition proceeded to LOOS under MAJOR MEAD and CAPT A.A. WINK via MAZINGARBE and PHILOSOPHE - Wagons proceeded in groups at 10 min. intervals and arrived at LOOS (Sq. 34 G. 5. 2.) about 9 p.m. Much difficulty was experienced in consequence of bad roads and mud covering shell holes. 24 wagons were unloaded and 12 wagons which could not be dealt with owing to the approach of daylight dumped their contents in PHILOSOPHE and all wagons returned to HESDIGNEUL between 4 am and 9 am on 4th.	
4/5	28 wagons with grenades and other ammunition taken under Capt WHITE	

Army Form C. 2118.

WAR DIARY
or
INTELLIGENCE SUMMARY

47th DIV. AMMUNITION COLUMN

(Erase heading not required.)

Hour, Date, Place	Summary of Events and Information	Remarks and references to Appendices
1915 Jan 4/5 HESDIGNEUL	Proceeded to MAROC via LES BREBIS arriving at 8 p.m. and returned by same on 5th. CAPT. CLARKE with 10 G.S. wagons proceeded to PHILOSOPHE and picked up ammunition dumped there previous night and carried it to INFANTRY BRIGADE dumps at LOOS returning to HESDIGNEUL by 8 a.m. on 5th. The work carried out on 2 nights of 3/4 and 4/5 Jan was in consequence of the LOOS front being taken by the British Army and the necessity of supplying the front line with reserve ammunition. 6. The train being 100 men under strength memo on the subject forwarded to 47th DIV. ARTY pointing out the difficulty of carrying out work and looking after horses in addition to the undertaking of drawing the lines. 7. 1/18 pr portion of Nº 3 Section 15th D.A.C. reported here that leaving Howitzer portion of section only	

Army Form C. 2118.

47th DIV. AMMUNITION COLUMN

WAR DIARY
or
INTELLIGENCE SUMMARY
(Erase heading not required.)

Instructions regarding War Diaries and Intelligence Summaries are contained in F.S. Regs., Part II. and the Staff Manual respectively. Title pages will be prepared in manuscript.

Hour, Date, Place	Summary of Events and Information	Remarks and references to Appendices
1916 Jan 7 HESDIGNEUL	Nos 1 & 2 Sections 10th D.A.C. attached to supply 1/1st London and 1/2nd London F.A. BDES	
" 8	45 men from 5th 6th 7th and 8th LON. F.A. BDES attached pending arrival of reinforcements	
" 11	Owing to shortage of hay, the issue of forage is temporarily reduced to 6lbs of hay per horse daily.	
" 14	Major Harold Hale, Staff Capt. 47 Div. Arty. took over command of 47 D.A.C. from Major H.L. Breade.	
" 13	47 O.Rs. arrived from Base, as reinforcements for 5th, 6th, 7th & 8th Lon. Bde. R.F.A.	
" 18	Major H.L. Breade left for England with orders to report to War Office.	
" 21	F.G.C.M. held at Column H.Q's re 2/Lt. Woodcock. 47th D.A.C.	
" 22	4 O.R's. despatched to 6th Lon. Bri. R.F.A. & 9 O.R's to 8th Lon. Bri. R.F.A. as reinforcements	
" 24	Lt. R.F. Tomlinson, 8th Lon. Bri. R.F.A. reported for duty & is posted to No 4 Section. Capt. C.C. White is posted from No 4 Section to No 3 Section	

Army Form C. 2118.

WAR DIARY
of
INTELLIGENCE SUMMARY

(Erase heading not required.)

47th Divisional Ammunition Column

Hour, Date, Place	Summary of Events and Information	Remarks and references to Appendices
1916.		
January 26th	50 recruits, including 45 on leave arrived & taken on strength.	
	Capt: E.S. Clarke, Adjt: 47th D.A.C. reported to H.Q. 47th Brd Arty for temporary duty	
	Capt: C.C. White posted Acting Adjt: during temporary absence of Capt: E.S. Clarke	
" 27	35 O.R's. reinforcements arrived from Base	
	Major H. Hale. posted to O.C. A.A. of 47 D.A.C	
" 28	15 O.R's. despatched to 5th Lon. Bri. A.S.C., 6 O.R's to 6th Lon. Bri. A.S.C.	
	5 O.R's. " " 7th " " & 6 O.R's " " 8th " "	
" 30	Divine Service (C.O.E.) held at 5.30 p.m. in mens tents	

Harold Hall
Major
Lt. Colonel Commanding
London Divisional A.M.M. Column (T.F.)

47

Div Am Col

Vol IX &
~~XI~~

WAR DIARY of 47th Divisional Ammunition Army Form C. 2118
Column
INTELLIGENCE SUMMARY for the month of February, 1916

(Erase heading not required.)

Place	Date	Hour	Summary of Events and Information	Remarks and references to Appendices
HESDIG-NEUL	2/2/16		Lieut. K. Harvey (attached from 8th Brigade) returned to that Brigade. 2/Lieut. G.A.E. Paterson joined on attachment from 8th Bgde. F.A. Brigade & was posted to No. 4 Section.	
do	3/2/16		Lieut. R.G. Tomlinson posted to No. 3 Section	
do	4/2/16		Draft of 46 other ranks arrived from Base.	
			30 other ranks (attached from 8th [—— F.A. Bde.) returned to that Brigade.	
			Howitzer portion of a section of 34th D.A.C. comprising 1 Sergeant, 13 other ranks, 1 riding horse, 20 mules, 2 wagons & 176 rounds 18× ammunition returned to attachment to 47th D.A.C.	
do	10/2/16		Field General Court Martial on No. 307 Dvr. H.K. Bambia, No.1 Section.	
do	17/2/16		47th D.A.C. less No. 3 Section and portion of No. 4 Section, moved into rest at AUCHEL occupying huts evacuated by 1st D.A.C.	
			No. 3 Section & portion of No. 4 Section referred to, attached to 1st D.A.C. & remained at HESDIGNEUL	
			Draft of 46 other ranks for ammunition artillery (including 11 for D.A.C.) arrived from Base.	
AUCHEL	21/2/16		Course of instruction in riding training by B.S.M. Wright, for 40 Infantry Brigade commenced.	
			Course of musketry training for D.A.C. commenced	

Army Form C. 2118

WAR DIARY of 4th Provisional Ammunition Column
INTELLIGENCE SUMMARY
Volume II February 1916
From 26/1/16 to 29/1/16
(Erase heading not required.)

Place	Date	Hour	Summary of Events and Information	Remarks and references to Appendices
AUCHEL	26/1/16		2 Officers, 80 other ranks & 80 horses of No 1 Section attached to 5th Lon F.A.Bde for manoeuvres in divisional Artillery manoeuvre area.	
do	28/1/16		Riding course for Officers of the Column commenced. 2/Lt D.S. Cottrell joined from Base, & posted to No 2 Section.	
do	29/1/16		Riding course for Junior N.C.O.s & drivers commenced.	

Murdoch
Lieut. Col.
Commanding, 4 F.P.A.C.

Army Form C. 2118.

WAR DIARY
INTELLIGENCE SUMMARY
(Erase heading not required.)

Instructions regarding War Diaries and Intelligence Summaries are contained in F.S. Regs., Part II. and the Staff Manual respectively. Title pages will be prepared in manuscript.

Hour, Date, Place	Summary of Events and Information	Remarks and references to Appendices
1916.		
March 1st. In the field.	Draft of 26 O.R's. arriving from the Base for Gnl. duty.	
" 2 " " "	Re-column Verg: Major commenced training 140 Inf. Bri: no firing still.	
" 4 " " "	N°.1 Section rejoined the Unit from manoeuvre area.	
" " " "	Musketry training commenced on rifle range.	
" 6 " " "	N°.2 Section carried out route march.	
" 8 " " "	Unit (less N°.3 Section) portion of N°.4 Section, attached to 2nd D.A.C.) moved from BRUAY to AUCHEL to new billeting area at BRUAY.	
" 15 " " "	N°.3 Section portion of N°.4 Section rejoined the Unit.	
" 17 " " "	Reconnaissance scheme carried out by Officers & N.C.O's.	
" 20 " " "	Unit moved from BRUAY to new billeting area at CAUCOURT.	
" 21 " " "	LT. G.R.E. STEPHENSON, rejoined the LON. (HOW) BRI.	
" 22 " " "	Unit moved from CAUCOURT to new billeting area at MAGNICOURT.	
" 23 " " "	LT. W.J. O'MALLEY attached to 7th LON: BRI: for instruction. LT. K. WEBSTER from 8th LON: (HOW) BRI: attached for duty.	

47

Div Amn Col

Vol X

XI

Army Form C. 2118.

WAR DIARY
INTELLIGENCE SUMMARY
(Erase heading not required.)

Instructions regarding War Diaries and Intelligence Summaries are contained in F. S. Regs., Part II. and the Staff Manual respectively. Title pages will be prepared in manuscript.

Hour, Date, Place	Summary of Events and Information	Remarks and references to Appendices
1916.		
March 26th In the field	Lt. D.S. CATTERALL attached to 7th LON: BRI: R.F.A. for instruction.	
" " "	Lt. W.J. O'MALLEY rejoined the unit.	
" 27th " "	Lt. BLAKE attached to 6th LON: BRI: R.F.A. " "	
" " "	Capt. F.J. CLARKE " " 8th " (HOW) " "	
" " "	Two 18 pdr: guns & two 4.5 howitzers attached from 2nd Bri: Arty: for instructional purposes.	
" " "	Capt. E.C. WHITE, attached to 8th LON: (HOW) BRI: for instruction.	
" " "	Capt. L.C. BARRY " " 5th " " " "	
" " "	Capt. F.J. CLARKE rejoined the unit.	
" 29th " "	Lt. D.S. CATTERALL " "	
" 30th " "	36 L.D. horses received from 23rd D.A.C.	
" " "	D.D.V.S. 1st ARMY, with A.D.V.S. 47th DIV: inspected the horses & mules of the unit.	

Jno Whitehale Lt: Col:
O.C. 47th D.A.C.

Army Form C. 2118

WAR DIARY
INTELLIGENCE SUMMARY
(Erase heading not required.)

Volume I

47th Divisional Ammunition Column

for month of April 1916

From 1/4/16 to 27/4/16

Place	Date	Hour	Summary of Events and Information	Remarks and references to Appendices
MAGNI-COURT	1/4/16		47th D.A.C. establishment brought up to establishment provisional armament shown for New Armies	Polk Norm Establ - Pt VIII New Armies
do	2/4/16		41 H.D. horses sent to Remount Depot, BONNEHEM	
do	3/4/16		Capt. L. C. Barry rejoined after attachment to 1st London F.A. Bde.	
do	4/4/16		G.O.C. Lectures by O/C Commander at GRAND SERVINS. S.O.ff Jaggard, K. Noble, & Lt. Cottrell attended.	
do	5/4/16		39 H.D. horses despatched to Remount Depot, CALAIS	
do	10/4/16		Entrenched in the Reserve trenches near by No 1 Section.	
do	14/4/16		1 N.C.O. & 13 other ranks proceeded for 8 days course instruction in Mortars Trench & plain	
do	16/4/16		Lt. G. A. McCook & 2/Lt. C.M. Keeler proceed from Base to new posts to No 3 and No 1 Sections respectively.	
do	17/4/16		3 Returning Horse Commander at GRAND SERVINS – Capt Clarke Barry Service observation, No 6 Hily attended	
do	24/4/16		Inspection by B.G., R.A., & Division.	
do	27/4/16		26 other ranks, 47 horses & 6 G.S. wagons attached to 4) 47 DAC from "R" Batteries, 5th, 6th, & 7th London AA Brigades	

Hanbury Lieut. Col.
O/c 47th D.A.C.

47

Volume I

WAR DIARY 1/47th Divisional Ammn Column Army Form C. 2118
or
INTELLIGENCE SUMMARY
(Erase heading not required.)

From 1/5/16 to 25/5/16

1/47th Divisional Ammn Column for the month of MAY 1916
Vol 12

Place	Date	Hour	Summary of Events and Information	Remarks and references to Appendices
MAGNICOURT	1/5/16	—	Opening of 1/47th Divl Artillery School of Instruction attached to 47th Divl Command — Lt Col H Hale; Instructor Capts P.J. Clarke & T. DE WITT	
do	8/5/16	9am	11th Officers & 15 N.C.O's of L'd Corps Artillery arrive, Brig Dunne Reader.	
do	9/5/16	9am	School of L'd Corps Artillery arrive. Capt R.A. work of No 2 Section, proceed to B.O.S. = B.A.A. work at various to B.O.S. = DE WITT	
do	10/5/16	—	Remainder of No 2 Section has no open details in connection with XVII Corps to work off riding	
do	11/5/16	—	Visit of Corps Commander, Lt Gen Sir H.A. Wilson, K.C.B., D.S.O.	
do	17/5/16	—	Capt & Adjt 4th Centre proceed to England for appointment to command of teams the T.F. BANK	
do	20/5/16	—	Lahie or "Trench Mortars" by Capt Byran, 2nd Divisional Artillery	
ONCOURT	21/5/16	—	Column 5th, 6th, 7th & 8th Brigade Ammunition Columns absorbed by 47th DAC	
do	22/5/16	—	An re-organisation of ammunition supply of 47th Div.	
			Column has details No 2 section lent to CA.C.O.V. R.T.	
			Column has extending supply units rapidly to brigade supply, trench supply with re-organisation finally on smaller scale. Columns heretofore with	
			formed Column commanded — Capt. R.G. Tomlinson	
			No 1 section — Capt. H.H. Pollock (from 5th B.A.C.)	
			No 2 — Capt. C.N. Bolton Hamilton (Army 7 B.A.C.)	
			No 3 — Capt. A.P.A. Knott	
			No 4 —	
do	22/5/16 25/5/16	—	Heavy ammunition supplies aimd 75,000 rounds live ammunition and 1¾ million rounds of S.M.A. handed by Column being bottle question	

WAR DIARY

Army Form C. 2118

Volume II
26/5/16 to 31/5/16

of 47th Divl. Ammunition Column Army
for month of MAY 1916

Place	Date	Hour	Summary of Events and Information	Remarks and references to Appendices
LAUCOURT	26/5/16	—	The divn. in having been relieved by 2nd Bde. Division, the Column less No.1 Section (re-organised) returned to MAGNI Coy d RF. No.1 section remained at CAUCOURT attached to 2nd DAC. Brought batteries of 47th Divn remaining in action with 2nd Divn in.	
MAGNICOURT	28/5/16	—	Work of re-organisation continued. Re-organisation continued. Three ammunition depots of S.A.A., 1st Army Affairs (24 hrs) & 100 other rounds despatched to VILLERS-AU-BOIS for on ordering party.	
do	30/5/16	—	127' horses & 2 mules sent by order of A.D.T.T. HQ AAC sent to southern Group of 230 Battery having been ordered into action with Division to reform from No.3 Section (Section A) proceeded to HUCHIN for attachment to section A 1st B.A.C. to supply the battery	
do	31/5/16	—	Work of re-organisation proceeding	

Randolph Lt. Col.
O.C. 47th D.A.C.

WAR DIARY

Army Form C. 2118

Volume I — No. 5 Brigade Ammunition Column
1/6/16 to 16/6/1 — INTELLIGENCE SUMMARY for the month of June 1916

Place	Date	Hour	Summary of Events and Information	Remarks and references to Appendices
MAGNICOURT	1st	—	1 G.S. wagon with accompanying personnel, horses & ammunition from N/5 Section ("B" Echelon) proceeded to HESDIGNEUL for attachment to "B" Echelon, 1st D.A.C. 6 empty C/235 Battery supply vehicles conveyed upon re-organisation expected to return (BRUAY)	
do	3rd		64 Remounts (Mules) collected from GONNEHEM bringing this returned from VILLERS-AU-BOIS	
do	5th		Re-organisation of Column complete	
do	7th		S.A.A. Portion of No.1 Section rejoined from CAUCOURT	
do	9/10		Baggage party went out cleaning to PRESNICOURT	
do	11th afternoon			
do	13th		28 Pick 7/6 Mules attached to 235 Brigade R.F.A. 32 Remounts (mules) collected from BRUAY 16 were attached D/236 Battery 16 were attached to Hospital 16 unknown attached	
do	10th		Column has 6 infantry bombs & bedding and 2 G.S. wagons & M.W. Section attached to 2 Batteries 2nd D.A. wires to BARLIN. Retained wagons attached M/236 Batty & R/236-236 Batteries detailed portion of No.3 cy Section rejoined from 1st D.A.C.	
do	16th	6 am		

Wt. W593/826 1,000,000 4/15 J.B.C. & A. A.D.S.S./Forms/C. 2118.

WAR DIARY or INTELLIGENCE SUMMARY

Army Form C. 2118

Volume II /JJK Divisional Ammunition Column
1/6/16 to 29/6/16 for the month of June 1916.

Place	Date	Hour	Summary of Events and Information	Remarks and references to Appendices
BARLIN	17th		Working parties supplied to B.T.M.O.	
do	19th		12 G.S. wagons returned with rations, tents, shelters to A/223 Battery. Issues infantrymen stores	
do	20th		Coll Tomlinson attached C/236 Batty	
do	21st		Captn J. T. Bevan attached to A/223 Batty. Issues on attachment to 235 Brigade R.F.A	
do	22nd		Demonstration of parachute rockets	
do	23rd		2/Lieut Loveacrick to 235 Brigade R.F.A. Captn R.G. Tomlinson rejoined from 236 Brigade R.F.A	
do	25th		Ektelon A/B to B/223 Battery. Found on attachment to Column. Working park of 9 Spr - 75 O.R.s supplied to refying in telephone wire.	
do	26th		2/Lt G.S. Tombe found on attachment to Column from 236 Brigade R.F.A. 2/Lieutld Pinlin 2/M 4 dechrs rejoined from STELOI. Following officers posted:	
			2/Lt G. GRATBURN to BTM O from 236 Bde RFA	
			2/Lt E. A. M. B. WEST - to 236 Bde R.F.A. from DAC	
			2/Lt C. WHEELER - to 231 Bde R.F.A from DAC	
			2/Lt G.E.G. TOMBE posted to 231 Bde RFA	
do	27th		2/Lt GRATBURN detached for course at Trench Mortar School	
			Further personnel casualties upon regiments despatched to BASE	

Army Form C. 2118

WAR DIARY Volume II 47 "Kensington" Kensington
or 4th London Regiment
INTELLIGENCE SUMMARY 27/6/16 — 1 June 1916

(Erase heading not required.)

Instructions regarding War Diaries and Intelligence
Summaries are contained in F.S. Regs., Part II.
and the Staff Manual respectively. Title Pages
will be prepared in manuscript.

Place	Date	Hour	Summary of Events and Information	Remarks and references to Appendices
MARLIN	27	16 June	CAPT. J. I. BEEVOR posts to B/H.C. and reverts to rank of Lieutenant	
do	29		12 remounts collected from GONNEHEM.	

Hardcastle
Lieut Colonel
Cmdg 47th Bn

1875 Wt. W593/826 1,000,000 4/15 J.B.C. & A. A.D.S.S./Forms/C. 2118.

47th Divisional Artillery.

47th DIVISIONAL AMMUNITION COLUMN R.F.A.

JULY 1916.

WAR DIARY

Volume I

of 47th Divisional Ammunition Column

INTELLIGENCE SUMMARY for the week of July 1916.

Title Pages from 1/7/16 to 17/7/16

Vol 14

Place	Date	Hour	Summary of Events and Information	Remarks and references to Appendices
BARLIN	1/7/16	—	Inspection of knee mules by D.A.D.S. 1st Army. L/Cpl Blake attd B/235 Battery	
do	2/7/16	—	20 remounts (mules) received from Remounts, GONNEHEM. L/Cpl Blake returned from B/235 Battery	
do	3/7/16	—	Nervous attack of the strength in accordance with order D.A.D.R. ?/?/?? to have 17 mules (7 mules 170 knees) collected from Remounts, GONNEHEM	
do	5/7/16	—	M/Sgt Brown attd HQ 238 Bde RFA B/Officers: 2/Lt ??? attd horse, L/M ??, W/Sgt, P.S.Agar, S.E. Hendall, Gn. ???, 2/Lt ??, Daniels, 2/Lt A.K. Agar's extended hospital	
			Casualties: joint furniture as under:	
			L/Cpl Drake — 238 Bde	
			2/L Sgt Daniels — 238 "	
			2/L. Hendall — 235 "	
			L/Sgt Agar — 235 "	
do	10/7/16	—	L/Cpl Blake returned from 235 Bde; 1½ mules /mule joint furniture. Knees picked by B/235RFA as ?? Arty ?? (5 cups) attached for instruction to Arty work ??????	
do	11/7/16	—	No 1 Section 63 (RN) D.A.C. attached for instruction to No4 Sect/c D.S.A.C.	
do	16/7/16	—	6 other ranks 63 (RN) D.A.C. attd to Column for instruction	
do	17/7/16	—		

WAR DIARY or INTELLIGENCE SUMMARY

Army Form C. 2118

Volume II
1st Bn. An Chum
From 19/7/16 to
Rank 1 July 1916

Place	Date	Hour	Summary of Events and Information	Remarks and references to Appendices
BARLIN	24/7/16	-	Lt Jay returned from 33S Bde; Lt Yorville attached to 235 Bde.	
do	25/7/16	-	Capt. Oakely arrived from Bars.	
do	26/7/16	-	Column moves to BRUAY	
do	26/7/16	-	47 remounts from Divn in Collects from station BRUAY just to Brigade also to DAC. 176 to be held for Brigade	
do	27/7/16	-	Lt Mortimer joined 287 Bde	
do	29/7/16	-	2 chargers & 35 LD remounts collects at BRUAY station for Brigade	
do	30/7/16	-	Column left BRUAY at 1am marching via DIVION – DIEVAL – ST POL – ECOIVRES – LE – BOUCQ	
VACQUERIES LE-BOUCQ	31/7/16	-	N.E.	

[signature]
Lt Col
Cmg 47th R.F.A.

47th Divisional Artillery.

47th DIVISIONAL AMMUNITION COLUMN R.F.A.

AUGUST 1 9 1 6

Volume I

WAR DIARY of "47" Div¹ Am" Column Army Form C. 2118

of 47th Div: Am" Column

INTELLIGENCE SUMMARY

for month of August 1916

From 1/8/16 to 24/8/16

(Erase heading not required.)

Vol 15

Place	Date	Hour	Summary of Events and Information	Remarks and references to Appendices
VACQUERIE-LE-BOUCQ OCCOCHES	1/8/16	4pm	Column marched via FORTEL – BONNIERES – BARLY to OCCOCHES	
	1/8/16	9pm	2/Lt A.E.H. Goodchild joined Column.	
BCCOCHES	2/8/16	—	Capt. R.G. Tomlinson transferred to command B/235 Battery.	
OCCOCHES	5/8/16	—	Sections Nos 1, 2, & 3 detached from Column & attached for totals to 235, 236, & 236 Bdes R.F.A. respectively.	
		4.30am	H.Q. & Echelon B marched via OUTREBOIS – MEZEROLLES – AUXI-LE-CHATEAU to TOLLENT	
TOLLENT	5/8/16	11.50am	2/Lt Wallace joined Column.	
			Lt J.J. Beeson rejoined from 235 Bde R.F.A. Transfer to Command Mot Section vice Capt Tomlinson transferred.	
			Tactical exercises under direction of B.G.R.A.	
TOLLENT	9/8/16			
	9/8/16			
TOLLENT	10/8/16	7.30am	H.Q. & Echelon B marched via GENNE IVERGNY – LE PONCHEL – AUXI-LE-CHATEAU – PRUVILLERS – BERNAVILLE to BERNEUIL	
BERNEUIL	10/8/16	3pm		
BERNEUIL	11/8/16	6.30am	H.Q. & Echelon B marched via CANAPLES to NAOURS	
NAOURS	11/8/16 10.30am			
NAOURS	14/8/16	3pm	H.Q. Echelon B marched via FLESSELLES to AGNICOURT	
AGNICOURT	14/8/16	7.15pm	Lt Jay Blake attached B/235 Battery	

Volume II   Army Form C. 2118

WAR DIARY of 49th Div¹ Amm. Column
INTELLIGENCE SUMMARY for Month of August 1916.
(Erase heading not required.)

Instructions regarding War Diaries and Intelligence Summaries are contained in F.S. Regs., Part II. and the Staff Manual respectively. Title Pages will be prepared in manuscript.

Place	Date	Hour	Summary of Events and Information	Remarks and references to Appendices
AGNICOURT	13/8/16	—	Sections No 1, 2 & 3 rejoined Column for extend Tranfers. 29 recruits collected.	
AGNICOURT	14/8/16	3.30 am	Column marched via BAIZIEUX - HENENCOURT - MILLENCOURT to ALBERT relieving 23rd Div² Amm. Column. Reg'l. & Ammunition suppl. taken over at 12 noon.	
ALBERT	14/8/16	9 am	F.G.C.M. on No. 3202 Dr Stott of No 3 Section. Capt. W.S. Brickman joined from England	
ALBERT	19/8/16	—	2/Lt Catterall transferred to 237 Bde RFA	
ALBERT	2/8/16	—	2/Lt M.J. Blake, 2/Lt Yorville, transferred to 235 Bde RFA	
"	20/8/16	—	2/Lt G.W. Badrum transferred to 236 Bde RFA	
"	"	—	2/Lt Mentieman transferred to 237 Bde RFA	
"	"	—	2/Lt Kendall transferred to 238 Bde.	
"	"	—	2/Lt Daniel transferred to 238 Bde.	
"	24/8/16	—	F.G.C.M. on No.77934 Dr Banks - J.J. No 1 Section	
"	"	—	2/Lts J.J. Blower, W.B. Thompson, 2/Lt Redmore, C.M. Bedwell. H.R. Faber T.P. Renown & Pt. Cole joined from Base.	
"	27/8/16	—	2/Lt Jay transferred to 236 Bde RFA	
"	28/8/16	—	2/Lt Faber Penman attached to 236 Bde RFA	
"	29/8/16	—	Capt C. Sexton Karkurten attached to 236 Bde RFA	
"	"	—	2/Lt Cole transferred to 4) T.M.B. all were our 2/Lt W Hopkinson joined to 3 Sect.	

WAR DIARY 1/47th Div.n Amn Colmn

INTELLIGENCE SUMMARY. Sept 1st to Sept 10th 1916

first month of September 1916

Vol 16

Army Form C. 2118.

Places	Date	Hour	Summary of Events and Information	Remarks and references to Appendices
ALBERT	1/9/16	10am	Ammunition Refilling Pond marked by 3 Russian Officers.	
do	2/9/16	—	Capt. C. Egerton Wharton returned from attachment to 236 Bde RFA.	
		—	2/Lt BLAKER transferred to 235 Bde RFA.	
		—	2/Lt TABOR returned from attachment to 236 Bde RFA.	
do	3/9/16	—	2nd Lts BEDNALL & THOMPSON attached 236 Bde RFA for instruction.	
		—	2/Lts J.T. JOHNSON, T.J. FORSTER, 2/Lt JACQUES, J. GARNETT, L/S de CASTRO joined from 63rd (RN) D.A.	
do	5/9/16	—	2/Lt R. WEBB attached 237 Bde RFA for duty.	
do		—	2/Lt J. FORSTER attached 47 T.M.B.s for instruction.	
do	7/9/16	12·45p	Runs — Shells — no casualties	
		—	2/Lt BERRETT joined from Base.	
		—	30 horses & 26 mules remounts received.	
		—	2/Lt TABOR evacuated suffering from shellshock. Struck off strength (auth 47 SM C.G.431 of 19/9/16)	
do	9/9/16	—	2/Lt JACQUES attached 237 Bde RFA for duty.	
do	10/9/16	—	2/Lt THOMPSON BEDNALL rejoined from attachment to 236 Bde RFA.	
		—	2/Lts B.B. WALLACE & H.P. SKIDMORE attached 236 Bde RFA for instruction.	

Army Form C. 2118.

VOLUME II

WAR DIARY 1/4 T/RFA

INTELLIGENCE SUMMARY for the month Sept 1st to Sept 19th 1916

Place	Date	Hour	Summary of Events and Information	Remarks and references to Appendices
ALBERT	10/9/16	-	2/Lt STENARD, FOSTER, INGRAM, LUND, HIRST, GOATNAM, HINTON joined from 46 T/RFA.	
do	10/9/16	-	Ammn Refilling Pond work stop. Staff move to BECOURT WOOD (F.1.d) lines remaining at ALBERT.	
do	14/9/16	-	Capt P. OAKLEY returned to England.	
do	15/9/16	-	Capt H. SHELDON DICKASON reverts to rank of 2/Lt on rejoining 6/Bty. L⁴ W. C. STOCKTON attached 236 Bde RFA for duty. 2 Parties under 2/Lt STENARD THINTON under direction of Asst Vet commenced work to East rivers side HIGHWOOD	
do	16/9/16	-	2/Lt WALLACE posted to 23 B/Bde RFA & 2/Lt WEBB JACQUES to 237 Bde RFA 2/Lt LUND attached 33 Bde RFA for duty	
BECOURT WOOD	-	-	Guns moved up to BECURT WOOD. Rockets fired at Ammn Refilling Pond. 2/Lt MERRITT attaches 235 Bde RFA for duty.	
do	17/9/16	-	2/Lt GARNETT STENARD attached for duty to 236 Bde RFA respectively. Road making parties returned, having had 6 casualties due to prematures.	
do	18/9/16	-	2/Lt SKIDMORE rejoined from attachment 236 Bde RFA. JOHNSON attached 236 Bde RFA. Prematures.	

Army Form C. 2118.

WAR DIARY
or
INTELLIGENCE SUMMARY

VOLUME III
Sept 21st to
1916

September 1916

Place	Date	Hour	Summary of Events and Information	Remarks and references to Appendices
BECOURT WOOD	21/9/16	—	Capt I. MACKINNON RAMC sick to C.C.S. Lt. COLE RAMC from 4th Lowland Field Ambulance joined as temporary M.O.	
do	22/9/16	—	Pte. J. FORSTER rejoins from 9 T.M. Bs.	
			2/Lt CHADWICK & Lt D.G. THOMAS joined from 29th T.M.B.	
			2/Lt LUND assumed duties of Transport	
do	23/9/16	—	Capt L.C. BARRY proceeds on course of Heavy T.M.s	
			2/Lt CHADWICK attached 235 Bde RFA for duty.	
			18 mules & Rider (Chaps) reinforcements received.	
do	23/9/16	—	2/Lt A.S.G. COLTHURST joined from 29 T.M.B.	
do	24/9/16	—	2/Lt HASKELL joined from 29th T.M.B.	
do	24/9/16	—	Lt. JOHNSON rejoins from attachment 6-235 Bde RFA	
			2/Lt COLTHURST attd 235 Bde RFA 2/Lt HASKELL & 2/Lt THOMAS attd 235 Bde RFA all for duty.	
			2/Lt STEWARD assumed duties of Asst Bde Adjut.	
do	30/9/16	—	2/Lt GOATMAN attd 235 Bde RFA for duty.	

Army Form C. 2118

WAR DIARY
or
INTELLIGENCE SUMMARY

(Erase heading not required.)

VOLUME I. 1/10/16 to 14/10/16

4/tt. D.A.C.

Place	Date	Hour	Summary of Events and Information	Remarks and references to Appendices
BECOURT WOOD	1/10/16		2/Lt A.G. OWEN SMYTH, G.W. CUMMOCK, G.T. CROOK, J. McFARLANE joined from base	
"	2/10/16		2/Lts J. GARNETT 236B᾿ᵈᵉ, R.A. DERRETT 235B᾿ᵈᵉ, M.O. HASKELL 236B᾿ᵈᵉ, transferred to the various brigades as from 30/9/16.	
"	4/10/16		CAPTAIN L.C. BARRY rejoined from School of Mortars. 2/Lts G.T. CROOK, J. MACFARLANE attached 236th Brigade	
"	5/10/16		2/Lts J.D. GIBB, A. LAMP, joined from Base. 2ⁿᵈ LT A. MORTON COLE, rejoined from England	
"	7/10/16		LT W.S. DICKASON, rejoined from hospital	
"	8/10/16		Dr BRUCE tried by F.G.C.M.	
"	9/10/16		CAPTAIN LOVE transferred from 236th B᾿ᵈᵉ	
MAMETZ	9/10/16		2ⁿᵈ LTs CROOK, J. McFARLANE rejoined from 236th B᾿ᵈᵉ Remounts collected. H.Q. & Dump moved to MAMETZ. 2ⁿᵈ LT PEARSON transferred to England. CAPTAIN WHITE proceeded on leave. CAPTAIN I.W. MAC KINNON transferred to England	
"	13/10/16		LT FORSTER attached 236th B᾿ᵈᵉ. H.Q. DUMP moved back to BECOURT	
BECOURT	14/10/16		Column moved from Becourt to BEHENCOURT	

Army Form C. 2118

WAR DIARY
or
INTELLIGENCE SUMMARY
(Erase heading not required.)

Instructions regarding War Diaries and Intelligence Summaries are contained in F. S. Regs., Part II. and the Staff Manual respectively. Title Pages will be prepared in manuscript.

Place	Date	Hour	Summary of Events and Information	Remarks and references to Appendices
BENENCOURT	15/10/16		Column moved from Benencourt to MOULLIENS	
MOULLIENS	16/10/16		Column moved from Moulliens to ORVILLE	
ORVILLE	17/10/16		Column moved from Orville to VACQUERIE LE BOUCQ	
VACQUERIE LE BOUCQ	18/10/16		Column moved from Vacquerie le Boucq to ANVIN	
ANVIN	19/10/16		Column moved from Anvin to (THEROUANNE)	
			Lt. Dickenson evacuated to England	
THEROUANNE	22/10/16		Column moved from Therouanne to ST. JAN-TER-BIEZEN	
ST JAN-TER-BIEZEN	22/10/16		2 Lts MACFARLANE, OWEN SMYTH attached 236th Bde	
			No 3 Section moved to new area in action at 6-9-d	
			2Lt DE CASTRO to Field Amb	
BUSSEBOOM	23/10/16		H.Q. and 1.2 sections moved to new area in action near BUSSEBOOM	
	24/10/16		No 3 section moved to lines adjoining No. 1.2 sections	
			No 4 Section moved to lines near WESTAUTREBEEK.	

Army Form C. 2118

WAR DIARY
or
INTELLIGENCE SUMMARY

(Erase heading not required.)

Volume III   23rd/10/16 to 29/10/16

Instructions regarding War Diaries and Intelligence Summaries are contained in F. S. Regs., Part II. and the Staff Manual respectively. Title Pages will be prepared in manuscript.

Place	Date	Hour	Summary of Events and Information	Remarks and references to Appendices
BUSSEBOOM	29/10/16		2nd Lts BEDNALL, LAMY, HIRST attached to 235th Brigade T.M. have evacuated by A.D.V.S. from WIPPENHOEK siding.	
"	29/10/16		66 reinforcements arrived for H.T.M. Battery.	

Harold Wake
Lt. Col.
O/C 47th D.A.C.

Army Form C. 2118

WAR DIARY or INTELLIGENCE SUMMARY
(Erase heading not required.)

of 47th D.A.C. for the month of Nov 1916

Instructions regarding War Diaries and Intelligence Summaries are contained in F.S. Regs., Part II. and the Staff Manual respectively. Title Pages will be prepared in manuscript.

Place	Date	Hour	Summary of Events and Information	Remarks and references to Appendices
BUSSEBOOM	1/11/16		2/Lt A. J. Owen Smyth to No 10 C.C.S.	
	2		2/Lt G. De Bastro, G. W. Bummock, G. T. Brook, attached 236th Bde. 2/Lt J. Forster attached 236th Bde. to Field Amb. Horse inspection by D.D.V.S. 2nd Army. Col. H. P. Skidmore attd. Y/47, T.M.B., Yds. S. W. Wells, L.E. Hinton to 2nd Army School of Mortars. Lt. D. G. Thomas transferred to 236 Bde.	
	3		19 Remounts taken on strength	
	4		Captain Barry unwell	
	5		Inspection of horses unfit for Artillery work by D.D.R. 2nd Army. Captain Wink to Field Amb.	
	7		2/Lt Forster, 2/Lt Macfarlane, De Bastro, Bummock, Brook, Goodman, Bednark reported from attachments to Bdes.	
	8		Inspection & distribution of horses by A.D.V.S. 2/Lt Forster, 2/Lt De Bastro, Goodman, Bednark transferred to 16th M. D.A.	
	9		F.G.C.M. on B.S.M. WEST & WAY	
	10		Capt Wink proceeded on leave. Yds Hinton & Wells rejoined from T.M. Course. 91 Mule remounts received	

Army Form C. 2118

WAR DIARY
or
INTELLIGENCE SUMMARY
(Erase heading not required.)

Place	Date	Hour	Summary of Events and Information	Remarks and references to Appendices
BUSSEBOOM	12/11/16		23rd L.D. horses evacuated. 2/Lt Horton transferred to X T.M.B.	
	13		2/Lt J.D. Gipp transferred to 60th D.A.	
	15		Lt. Col. H. Hale proceeded on leave. Capt T.C. White struck off strength	
	16		2/Lt Lorry and 15 O. Ranks proceeded on T.M Course	
	17		Capt E. Warburton proceeded to School at Shoeburyness.	
	18		2/Lt Montgomerie attached to A.237th Battery	
	21		2/Lt W.J. O'Malley proceeded on leave	
	23		2/Lt L.G. Owen Smyth struck off strength	
			Capt. Capt. Pollock returned from leave. 3 L.D. 25 mules collected	
	24		Capt Wind proceeded on leave. 2/Lts A.M. BOWN & L.N. MACKIE returned from base. 2/Lt Thompson attached C/235 Bg.	
			2/Lt Bown & Mackie attached Right Group.	
	25		2/Lt Weeks proceeded on leave. 2/Lt Blackwood struck off strength w.e.f. 23/11/16	
	26		Lt. Col. Hale returned from leave. 2/Lt Lorry returned from T.M. School.	

Army Form C. 2118

WAR DIARY
or
INTELLIGENCE SUMMARY
(Erase heading not required.)

26/11/16 to 30/11/16

Place	Date	Hour	Summary of Events and Information	Remarks and references to Appendices
BUSSEBOOM	26/11/16		Draft of 30 O.R.s arrived. 11 Mules collected from 236th Bde	
	27/		2/Lt Long attached Heavy T.M.B.	
	29		2/Lt M.J. O'Malley returned from leave	
	30		Captain Lord & Hony Webb joined from leave	
			F.G.C.M on Gunner Sgt Rowe.	

Harold Vidal Lt. Col.
47th D.A.C.

WAR DIARY or INTELLIGENCE SUMMARY

Army Form C. 2118.

Volume I 4th Dec /16 to 13/12/17

J D 19

Hour, Date, Place	Summary of Events and Information	Remarks and references to Appendices

BUSSEBOOM

Dec 1916
1. Capt. D. F. Lond & Maj. Webb attached 235th Bde
2. 2/Lt. Cavanagh att. T.M. Battery
3. Presentation of Standards by G.O.C. to 1st Canad. Presentation of Standards by G.O.C. to Lt. Harvey, Bdr. Lawrence, Dr. Lansbergh
4. 2/Lt. Ascroft, Capt. Low proceed on leave. Instructions received for Capt. Warburton to report on arrival to War Office. Personnel of X 47 T.M.B. moved to new billets at Righebogap H.Q.
5. 2/Lt. Wiles & Cammack marched. 83 teams out on ammunition & brick fatigue.
5. Lt. Cole M.O. to F.A.
6. 2/Lt. Ingram from Hospital
7. 2/Lt. W.G.B. Thompson from A/238 Battery 1st Bde. same rank
8. to leave
9. 2/Lt. Wheeler returned from leave
10. Dr. Johnson returned to duty
12. Capt. Mark returned from leave
13. Capt. Mark to Field Amb. 2/Lt. Dunlan evac to England

Volume II

WAR DIARY
or
INTELLIGENCE SUMMARY

Army Form C. 2118.

14/10/16

Hour, Date, Place	Summary of Events and Information	Remarks and references to Appendices
BUSSEBOOM Oct 14	Capt Lane & H.D. Johnson returned from leave	
15	G.O.C. Div inspected camp	
16	Lt Beever proceeded on leave	
17	H.D. Johnson to 311 Amb. Capt Blick away out of Div area. Lt Ettoman joined R.A.M.C. posted to this unit	
18	Capt J.J. Scanlan R.A.M.C. posted to this unit	
19	Lt Strachi came from Div train	
21	Capt Lane returned from leave. 235 Bde posted to No 3 section	
22	H.D. Johnson proceeded on leave	
23-24-5		
26	Somethin Bellman, Morton, Beltran joined from England. H.D. Sudan to No 3 sec & T M B for instruction	
27/5	Mellows, Beltran to No 3 Section & T.M.B. for instruction	
H.D. Balmoral to No 3 sec. Lecture & talk to troops	
Popering he 31 m Capt Jog Wells poster A235 Bdy	
together details to leave Enden Spade Work	
27	Lt Hopkinson joined from leave	
28	2nd Lt A/A Whit sec F. English	
29	Lut J S Burn arrived from Rouen 2Lt G N Mahon joined DAC	
30	Lieut P S Holl joined DAC	

WAR DIARY or INTELLIGENCE SUMMARY

Army Form C. 2118.

Volume I 1/1/17 to 16/1/17

217th D.A.C. Vol 20

Place	Date	Hour	Summary of Events and Information	Remarks and references to Appendices
BUSSEBOOM	1/1/17		2/Lt. D. Morton to be transferred to 236th Bde. Capt. Love 2/Lt. Ousley, Ballard & Martin attached to 2nd Army T.M. School. 2/Lt. Ballow attd. T.M. 2/Lt. Macfarlane trans. to 233 Bde.	
	2		Col. Hale attended conference of Div. Commanders at Div H.Q.	
	3		2/Lts. N.J. Foster, S.L. Ingram proceeded on leave.	
	4		18 O.Rs. arrived. Capt. Warburton struck off strength.	
	6		2/Lt. School trans. to Inf. Lieut. Dohen to have attd. T.M.	
	8		2/Lt. Elliott, 2/Lt. Ramsay joined D.A.C. R.S.M. Wright proceeded on leave. Lt. Houston, 2/Lt. Hay joined from leave. Lt. W. Hodgkinson rejoined from leave.	
	10		A.S. remounts collected.	
	11		Col. Hale attended conference at Div. H.Qrs.	
	13		2/Lt. Ballard to Hospital from T.M. School. 2/Lt. Foster from leave. Capt. Love 2/Lt. Ousley, Martin rejoined from T.M. school. Capt. Love posted to commence Div. section. 2/Lt. Martin attached T.M.B.	
	15		2/Lt. Thompson proceeded on leave.	
	16		2/Lt. Le May, 130 O.Rs. attached 2nd Army T.M. school. Capt. Walker posted to command No.1 section. 2/Lt. Elliott attd of 238 Batt. 2/Lt. Dohen proceeded on leave.	

Volume II 17/1/17 to 27/1/17

WAR DIARY
INTELLIGENCE SUMMARY
Army Form C. 2118.

41st D.A.C.

Place	Date	Hour	Summary of Events and Information	Remarks and references to Appendices
BUSSEBOOM	17		Inspection by Corps Commander, C.R.A. 2nd Lt Wale proceeded on leave. 2nd Lt De Wall rejoined. 2nd Lt Mackie transferred to 238th Bde.	
	18		Inspection by Army Commander. Present G.O.C. Division, C.R.A. 2nd Lt De Wedd posted to B/236th Bty. Lt F.S.W. Cranston 2nd Lt Romney transferred to 236th Bde. R.S.M. Wright from leave.	
	19			
	20		Orders given for Re-organisation. Lt Bean proceeded on leave.	
	21		Lt Col Ebury C.M.G. interim Commander. Lt George Capt 2nd Lt Whalley, Underwood Robinson, Harnett arrive from leave. 2nd Lt Hurst transferred to B/235 Bty. transferred to 169th B.A.C.	
			L/C Davies, Taylor, gunner from 236th	
	23		2nd Lt Miles gunner from 236th Bde	
	24		2nd Lt Lansley transferred to 236th Bde	
	25		2nd Lt Ron Jones, Capt Sarah transferred 169th Bde. Lt Oldfield to command No 1	
	26		2nd Lt Robinson transferred to 233rd Bde. 2nd Lt Elliott to 236th Bde. section.	
			2nd Lt Overton, Leslie, Davis, Tyler, & Everett from leave. Inspection by B.C.R.A. Corps	
	27		Draft of 29 O.R. from base. 10 horseworth collection. 2nd Lt Thompson from leave	

Volume III 29/1/17 to 31/1/17

Army Form C. 2118.

WAR DIARY
or
INTELLIGENCE SUMMARY.
(Erase heading not required.)

Instructions regarding War Diaries and Intelligence Summaries are contained in F. S. Regs., Part II. and the Staff Manual respectively. Title pages will be prepared in manuscript.

Place	Date	Hour	Summary of Events and Information	Remarks and references to Appendices
BUSSEBOOM	29		2/Lt Ingram rejoined from leave. 2/Lt George, bogue, 2/Lt Tyler and others transferred to 104th T.B.A.C.	
	30		2/Lt Le May from T M School. 2/Lt Leslie Davis transferred to 235th TMB	
			2/Lt Penrose joined.	
	31.		2/Lt Le May transferred to T.M.	

Stanley
Lt. Col.
Comdg 11/12 DAC

Army Form C. 2118.

Volume I
47th D.A.C.
Vol 21

WAR DIARY
or
INTELLIGENCE SUMMARY.
(Erase heading not required.)

Instructions regarding War Diaries and Intelligence
Summaries are contained in F. S. Regs., Part II.
and the Staff Manual respectively. Title pages
will be prepared in manuscript.

1/9/16
20/9/17

Place	Date	Hour	Summary of Events and Information	Remarks and references to Appendices
BUSSEBOOM	1/9/16		2/Lt Reeve to V.T.M.B. 2/Lt Bathurst posted to D.A.C. 2/Lt Stainous from leave	
	4/9/17		2/Lt. 28 OR Men from 104 Bde	
	6/9		3 Canadian in 2 T.M.B, all killed. 2/Lt Taylor proceed on leave	
	7/9		Capt Pemberton reports. 2/Lt Black joined from England	
	7/9		2/Lt Mills proceeded on leave	
	8/9		2/Lts Lamb, Stevens, Metcalfe, Stern, Millen, Mackenzie joined from England	
	9/9		2/Lt Owen transferred to England	
	10/9		2/Lt Mackenzie att X Corps Railways	
	11/9		2/Lt Black to Hospital	
	12/9		2/Lt McKay & M.G. att D.A. Capt Love assumes command	
	12/9		B/Vet Capt Dr Lock Blake hand in by F.G.C.M. 2/Lt. Stern to Hospital	
	14/9		2/Lt Oveston, Metcalfe att Left half 2/Lt Onesett, Lamb att Right Sep	
	15/9		2/Lt Whitty 14 days sick leave	
	16/9		3000 rounds 2" T.M. ammunition delivered to Convent dump by light railway	
	17/9		Capt Stewart A.V.C. to Hospital	
	20/9		2/Lt Balham wounded in action. B.S.M. Fisher from 45 R.H., R.F.A., transferred	

Army Form C. 2118.

Volume II   47th D.A.C.

WAR DIARY
or
INTELLIGENCE SUMMARY.

(Erase heading not required.)

21/2/17 to
28/2/17

Place	Date	Hour	Summary of Events and Information	Remarks and references to Appendices
BUSSEBOOM	21/2/17		Col. Foy assumed command from 47th D.A. HQ Orby T.M.B. known as 236 BS	
	23/2		2nd Lt. Underwood to Hospital	
	24		2nd Lt. Mills from leave	
	25		H/C Hethow from Hospital. Lt. Mills from Hospital. Capt. Barker joined. Lt. Col. Dale struck off strength	
	27		2nd Lt. Foy, Lt. Miller, RSM Laing left for England. Captain Lowe assumes command.	
	28		Lt. Romney reported from base and given 236 = Bde.	

Mackelvie Lt.
Capt 47th D.A.C.

Mackelvie Lt.
Capt 47th D.A.C.

WAR DIARY or **INTELLIGENCE SUMMARY** 47th - D.A.C.

Army Form C. 2118.

Volume I 1/3/17 to 24/3/17

Hour, Date, Place	Summary of Events and Information	Remarks and references to Appendices
BUSSEBOOM 1st March	2/Lt Lamb rejoined from Right Grup. 2/Lt Lamb to 2nd Army T.M. school	
3"	2nd Lt May, Shelton attached to Battery of M/staff from D/236 J/236 Order from 7/236	
4"	Monsieur de Beauvoir the tenant of the ground ₰ D.A.C. Officers Mess ascertain and	
4"	2/Lt Whitby rejoined from sick leave. 2/Lt Beaver arrived off overdraft	
7"	2/Lt Ballard over to England	
10"	2/Lt Black over to England	
13"	further details to home	
14"	2/Lt Taylor rejoined from leave	
14"	2/Lt G Nally att Y/47 to T.M.B.	
14"	2/Lt Taylor attached D/235 7/Lt Donnan + 2/Lt reposted	
15"	2/Lt Lamb rejoined from T.M. school 7/Lt Murray reported & posted to V/62	
16"	2/Lt Burton att T.M. School	
19"	2/Lt Col Allen reported	
20"	2/Lt Wickham off. of Hopkins	
21"	3 years of Service active service in France begins 4/4/16	
24"	2/Lt Ballard, Underwood Sanderson & Gilligan Joined Column	

WAR DIARY or INTELLIGENCE SUMMARY

Army Form C. 2118.

A.7 — D.A.C. 24/3/17 to 3/4/17

Hour, Date, Place	Summary of Events and Information	Remarks and references to Appendices
BUSSEBOOM 24th March	Lieut Gairs blown at 5:45 a.m. Lieut Taylor to No 4 section from D/235	
25 "	Capt. Stephen joined and posted to 2/5	
27 "	Lieut Overton to No 4 from D/235. Lieut McKay No 4 to D/235	
28 "	Lieut Glover attached Left front. Capt. McKay at T.M.	
29 "	Lieut Underwood attached Left front. Capt. Overton to Right front	
"	Lieut Overton from 2nd Army T.M. School	

M. Stephen Lieut
A/Lt A/7 — D.A.C.

WAR DIARY or INTELLIGENCE SUMMARY

Army Form C. 2118.

47th - D.A.C.

Hour, Date, Place	Summary of Events and Information	Remarks and references to Appendices
BUSSEBOOM 1st March	2/Lt Lamb rejoined from Right Sect. 2/Lt Lambt to 2nd Army T.M. school	
3rd	2/Lt Le May, Stellion attached to Battery 2/Lt Midcalf from D/236 J/47 Midcalf from D/236	
	Monsieur de Beaumon the [lord] of the manor	₂/236 J/47 B coloff from J/236
	2/Lt Whitby rejoined from sick leave	6 officers when enumerated and
	2/Lt Balfour error to England	J/L Beavers struck off strength
7th	2/Lt Black error to England	
10th	Surplus details to home	
13th	Lt. E. Taylor rejoined from leave	
14th	2/Lt E. Mallby att Y/47 TMB Sgt Donovan & VC reported	
	Lt Taylor attached D/235 75th Many reported transfer to No 2	
15th	2/Lt Lamb rejoined from T.M school	
16th	2/Lt Davies att T.M school	
19th	Lt. Col Allen reported	
20th	Lt. Mitchison appt of Captain as from 4/4/16	
21st	3rd Year of homes active service in France begins	
24th	2/Lt Balfour, Midcalf, Sandilands, Gilligan joined column	

Volume II

WAR DIARY
or
INTELLIGENCE SUMMARY

Army Form C. 2118.

A.7 - D.A.C. 24/3/17 to 3/4/17

(Erase heading not required.)

Hour, Date, Place	Summary of Events and Information	Remarks and references to Appendices
BUSSEBOOM 24th March	Fest Fire alarm at 5.45 A.M.	
25 "	Capt Younis Stephens served and ordered to Y.15	Section from D/233
27 "	2nd Lt. Overton to No.4 from D/233	
"	2nd Lt. Younis Stephens attd Left front.	No 4 to D/233
29 "	2nd Lt. Underwood attd Left front. Left Stephens att T.M.	
"	2nd Lt. Overton from 2nd Army T M School	Overton to Right front

M Stephens Lieut
A/Capt A.7 - D.A.C.

Volume I
47th - D.A.C.
April 1917
Vol 23

WAR DIARY or INTELLIGENCE SUMMARY
Army Form C. 2118.

(Erase heading not required.)

Place	Date	Hour	Summary of Events and Information	Remarks and references to Appendices
BUSSEBOOM	11/4/17		Cpl Brabner (970291) and Driver Brown (965448) answered Military Medal for gallantry at Brick Dump (H.24.a.9.5.) circumstances were as follows. On Sunday 25th March 1917 whilst Brabner & Brown were being heavily shelled by the enemy Cpl Brabner assisted by Dr. Brown organised a party of men and cut out the through the wall of a heavily shell. By this means to succeeded in the rescue of some mules belonging to the R.W. Fusiliers. By his energy he very considerably helped to limit the fire caused by enemy shells which became falling through the lens the cordite dump the event of which was at hazard.	
	14		New ammunition dump at H.13 centre taken over Draft of 35 Obrs & 7 Drs to Batteries	
	9		Fat. of 6 Horses killed in action by shell fire while at work	
	16		fr. Z[4] T.M.B. Captain Love proceeded on 1 months absence leave	

WAR DIARY or INTELLIGENCE SUMMARY

Volume II
47th D.A.C.
Army Form C. 2118

Place	Date	Hour	Summary of Events and Information	Remarks and references to Appendices
BUSSEBOOM	23		Lt. Floyd R.E. attached to No 2 Section for a week on locate in table management	
	25		TM's ammunition under supervision of OTMO from HQ only sent direct to D.A.	
	27		DAC made arrangements for supply of much for the empty. the ammunition light railway & officer 352 rounds and 88 rounds detailed for this fatigue. No 4 section ammunition heavy extract and [illeg] sheets, working parties an	
	28		TM component halts being discharged Grant dump 1429 9-3" 1187+ other 111. 9-45" bombs replaced moving a section in the dumb [illeg] moon wanes 12-45 dusk dawn 23ft arrows	
June	30		Differing schemes than A 1343 lbs than B 269 lbs than C 12 mtls in country without heavy 391 lbs Single Officers. Orderlies 819 horses, Mules 866.	

Mayflys/Lieut 47th D.A.C.

WAR DIARY or INTELLIGENCE SUMMARY

Army Form C. 2118.

Volume I 17th D.A.C. 1/5/17 to 31/5/17 Vol 24

Place	Date	Hour	Summary of Events and Information	Remarks and references to Appendices
BUSSEBOOM	1st		Capt Mitchener him to DAC from V/47 = TMB and rank to unit of Sav	
	2		Battery of Gun teams number 320 to.	
	3		Lieut Gilbert to Gun Park from fater 10.00 p.m.	
	5		Light Section RAMC. from civilian lines.	
	6		Horse lines No 2 horse detail arrived at OUDERDOM camp changed	
	7		No 2 to No 3 horse detail arrived till end of term at OUDERDOM Horse lines	
			2 mule wagons	
	10		D.A.C. attached dumping ammunition in X plow positions 22 mag an extensive	
	11	7.30 pm	amount of dumped supplies in X ashen positions from 360 to 70 team	
			went nightly total number of rounds dumped 69,000. 73 team hours	
			out 67. Mad fatigue on night of 26th	
	24		2/Lt Allen proceeded on leave	
	25		Column Office moved to dump at H 13 central sheet 28	
	27/6/31		Team took 12 batteries to take them ammunition to fire. Being	
			on all occasion on the 29th + 30th 13 mules were killed, 11 reported	
			and 11 drivers wounded by shell fire.	

Army Form C. 2118.

Volume 11   47th D.A.C.

WAR DIARY
or
INTELLIGENCE SUMMARY
(Erase heading not required.)

Place	Date	Hour	Summary of Events and Information	Remarks and references to Appendices
Sht 1-25 H 13 c	May		General.	
	1-26		During the month 50.B.2 men of men of mines to service at dumps from Sht.- Laboure Bonke. They are a very willing and keen body of men and every task has been without confusion.	
			R.E.'s Section of Army Field Coy 47 Div Bryals driven ammn from 47 Div A.R.P. and forwards the same to each of the B.A.C.'s. The work on dumps eg :- 14, 64, 86, 104, 119, AFA BAC. 20 to end of month amounts of rounds handled average 18 to 25 thousand per day. Monthly men employed on dumps 140 compared as follows DAC 40, AFA BAC 50, AFA BAC 50, Labour 50.	
			Drafting returned during month. Have A 562 b. Han B. 351 bb Han 12 mth in country and have to leave 475 Horses, Mules. 843 Strength Officers, Branks. 779	

M..ghun ..
Lt/Col 47. DAC

WAR DIARY
or
INTELLIGENCE SUMMARY

Army Form C. 2118.

Volume I 1/6/17 No 11/6/17

47th D.A.C.

Vol 25

Place	Date	Hour	Summary of Events and Information	Remarks and references to Appendices
SHEET 28 H 13.c	1st		Continuous fire from Heavies. Casty of 41 OR under an Officer from 82 L.D. wounds	
	3		Dump shelled at 1 hour enemies from 9 p.m. to 5 a.m. 4/6/17. Dump of Grenades not on fire but fire extinguished by prompt action of the picket and dump staff. The baskets ammunition was under M.M. fire above all. Harness ag. every dump of only Wagons by enemy shell fire	
	4		Remount Officer by reason from leave takes 23 attached to D.A.C.	
	5		Lt. Col. Allen rejoined from leave	
	6		Capt. H.H. Schock awarded M.C. on occasion of King's Birthday for War Services	
	7		Attack for the capture of the heights commenced about 3.10 a.m. 2nd Lt. G.H. Ward slightly wounded. Lt. E.J. Underwood attached T.M.B. died of wounds received in action	
	11		10 ORs sent as a draft to 235 - T. Bde	

Army Form C. 2118.

WAR DIARY
or
INTELLIGENCE SUMMARY.

Volume II   47th D.A.C.

13/6/17 to 30/6/17

(Erase heading not required.)

Instructions regarding War Diaries and Intelligence Summaries are contained in F. S. Regs., Part II. and the Staff Manual respectively. Title pages will be prepared in manuscript.

Place	Date	Hour	Summary of Events and Information	Remarks and references to Appendices
LA CLYTTE	13		Column Officer moved to near La Clytte at Sheet 28 N.1.a.8.d. No.1 Section to G.36 at 6-8. No.2 Section G.35.c.8-7. No.3 Section remained at old lines at G.33 d 9-3. The D.A remain in action and draws ammunition from 41st dump at N4 c 4.4. 7th Divisions and 25 O.R's attached to 41st dump.	
	14		47th A.R.P at H.13 central handed over to 30th D.A.C.	
	15		Dump of 13th O.R.S No. 235 - Bde. 2 British Balloons seen to come down in flames outposts of one believed by enemy balloon coming in contact with the parachute on the descent.	due to enemy heat
	17		100 men attend Church Parade at 2.35 - W.Ko. 9 A.M. D = Brown Service with H.M returned by C.R.A.	
	18		1 days promotion on leave	
	23		2 British Balloons brought down in flames by hostile plane 1-30 p.m. Bomb dropped on Reinghelst by hostile plane.	
	24		Hostile plane flew very low over La Clytte 11 am	
	27		Two British Balloons brought down in flames by hostile plane	
	29		26 reinforcements to 235 - Bde	
	30		Major returned from leave	

W. D. Young Lieut & D.A.
Adjt 47th

Volume I July 1st
          July 31st

WAR DIARY
or
INTELLIGENCE SUMMARY

Army Form C. 2118.

47th D.A.C.

Vol 26

Hour, Date, Place	Summary of Events and Information	Remarks and references to Appendices
LA CLYTTE 1917		
1st	Enemy busy shelling back areas, few fell in HQ camp area. Dump at MN4c2.2 taken over from 41st D.A.C.	
2nd	A second dump for horsed ammunition commenced at LA CLYTTE. 2nd Lt M.G. BLACK reported and placed in charge of La Clytte dump.	
4th	Enemy planes dropped bombs in neighbourhood, one fell in No 1 Section's lines wounding Lop Cooks Kilvenin, 2 O.R.s.	
5th	Gnrs Burkett, Danzy, Falconer, 1 Dr Ware reported in orders as having been awarded the M.M. for gallantry on 26/3/17. (x Batt R.O. 1222)	
	H.M. the King inspected Dressing + Evacuation trench working system x batt along La Clytte – Reninghelst R.	
		RAMC
5th	Capt J.F. Scanlan to 5 Fd. Amb., Capt M.J.C. Slattery from RAMC added for duty	
	Capt J. Fayle to X Battery for duty. Capt R. Bogden A.V.C. attached	

Volume II
July 8th
July 17

47th - D.A.C. Army Form C. 2118.

WAR DIARY
or
INTELLIGENCE SUMMARY
(Erase heading not required.)

Hour, Date, Place	Summary of Events and Information	Remarks and references to Appendices
LA CLYTTE 8th	Column H.Q moved to N 4 c.30 sheet 28	1st Echelon moved to N 4 B centre
DICKEBUSCH LAKE 9th	7 W.W. Shietman took charge of La Clytte dump	
11th	2 Hostile planes attacked, fired three of our balloons	
12th	Hostile plane flew low over camp, fired on M.G on road 10p.m.	
16th	Hostile plane dropped bombs on Australian horse lines in field adjoining H.Q killing 34 animals & wounding 17, three of shells fell on dump	
17th	Hostile plane brought one of our balloons down in flames within two fields of dump	
	2.45 (Capt S.O) W. Hayhurst, 7845, H.J. Foster, T. Ballangie joined units on T. F with Precedence as from 1/6/16	

VOLUME III 47th D.A.C.
July 19th to July 29

WAR DIARY or INTELLIGENCE SUMMARY
Army Form C. 2118.

(Erase heading not required.)

Hour, Date, Place 1917	Summary of Events and Information	Remarks and references to Appendices
DICKEBUSCH LAKE 19th	About 2 AM shell fell into dump without causing damage to the dump & both mens.	
LA CLYTTE 22nd	H.Q. moved to La Clytte dump handed over to 47th D.A.C.	
24th	47th mule remounts arrived	
27th	Hostile plane; flare dropped at 10 P.M.	
	two fell in No. 4 Section's lines killing 18 mules	
28th	Hostile plane about 10 P.M. Flare bomb own district dropping bombs	
29	Gas alarm sounded about 2 AM Gas was very faint.	
General	Work during month consists generally of fatigues and on average of 40 wagons of ammunition per night taken to gun positions. 19,460 Rounds of ammunition delivered to Batteries during the period 4th to 22nd.	

M/Lt Henry Tayler 47th D.A.C.

Volume I 1/6/17 to 47th D.A.C. Army Form C. 2118.

WAR DIARY
or
INTELLIGENCE SUMMARY.
(Erase heading not required.)

47th D.A.C. 11/6/17

Hour, Date, Place	Summary of Events and Information	Remarks and references to Appendices
LA CLYTTE Aug 1	2/Lt M.S. Black, F.P. Jones proceeded on T.M. course	
4	20 Reinforcements to 235th Bde, Lytham Wick attached	6/190 B5
5	10 Reinforcements to 235th Bde	
7	Lt Col G.T. Seward posted to 37th Div HQ	
8	2/Lt Long, L. Wheeler again from leave	
	Major R.H. Pollock proceeded on leave	7/4-G.T. McKinnon
9	proceeded with party to Calais to collect remounts	
10	Enemy attack with 9.2", 11" avoids of Acclear lines, hostile aircraft dropped bombs on district during any Div	
	65 Reinforcements arrived from Base	
11	29 Reinforcements arrived from Base	

Feleron II 12/8/17 to   47th D.A.C.

Army Form C. 2118.

WAR DIARY
or
INTELLIGENCE SUMMARY.
(Erase heading not required.)

Instructions regarding War Diaries and Intelligence
Summaries are contained in F.S. Regs., Part II.
and the Staff Manual respectively. Title pages
will be prepared in manuscript.   10/9/17

Hour, Date, Place	Summary of Events and Information	Remarks and references to Appendices
LA CLYTTE Aug 12	Hostile aircraft attempt attacked front 1 Balloon,	7.35 Machinegun returned
	with remnants 11 Patrol to Balloon.	
13	Hostile Plane at 11.30am dropped bomb on No 2 Lechery horse	
	wounding 3 O.R's (three), 2 L.D. Walker 3 L.D. wounded	
14	Reinforcements from Zone	
15	Reinforcements to 235 Bde. Hostile plane attacked Balloon	
	our times destroyed.	
15	At 3pm a formation of 7 hostile planes dropped bombs on	
	Dickebusch.	
16	Hostile planes over at 10pm Bombs dropped	
17	" " " " " "	
18	" " " " " "	
19	" " 9.30-10pm " " "	

Volume III 19/8/17

WAR DIARY
or
INTELLIGENCE SUMMARY.
(Erase heading not required.)

Army Form C. 2118.

47th – D.A.C.

Title pages 30/8/17

Hour, Date, Place		Summary of Events and Information	Remarks and references to Appendices
LA CLYTTE	July 19	Belgian Interpreter Monsieur Davreys rejoined.	
	20	Hostile planes over again 9 pm to 10 pm took shelter.	
		Hostile attack from German	
	21	Billeting parties under Major to Boeschepe	
	22	Echelon moved to Boeschepe there on R.5.a. Hy.Hy Shock falls	
BOESCHEPE		to D/235 Bty.	
	24	Lt. Foster proceeded on leave. 2nd Army lorries	
		inspected & ect'n in their lines at 11 am	
		Lt. Nunn Foster as Officer i/c A.R.P.	
REMINGHELST	29	Mobilization moved to new lines H.Q. G.20.B.3.3.	Nos. 3 & 19.D.1-4.
		No. 2. G.15 central.	No. Gp.H –
	30	Rejoin Wick & signed from 41st D.A.	G.M.-
			F. DAC.
			M. Morton Maj. R.F.A.

Volume I 1/9/17 to

47th D.A.C.

Army Form C. 2118.

Vol 28

WAR DIARY
or
INTELLIGENCE SUMMARY
(Erase heading not required.)

Place	Date	Hour	Summary of Events and Information	Remarks and references to Appendices
HOOGRAAF	2		Enemy planes dropped bombs during night 2nd-3rd	
	3		S.A.A. Section rejoined. Enemy planes over during the night many bombs dropped. Gunner Walker 23 wounded. Lieuts & Walker	
			Put in charge of Salvage	
	4		Lt. F. Illingworth rejoined and posted to No.1 Section. G.F. Hamendorf landed over to 25th Div. Enemy planes over 4 & 5th many bombs dropped. Lt. Gaunter returned on ambulance on medical grounds	
	5		Enemy planes over. 1 man wounded by anti aircraft gun shrapnel Bydann. Wick tip trucks collected 26 remounts from Mikkelnoek	
	6		No 4 Section moved to new lines G21a 2-6. Very hard storm during every	
	7		G.O.C inspected Schema horse lines during morning. Enemy planes dropped bombs during night.	
	8		Enemy planes over during night	
	10		21 D. Informants arrived. Enemy planes over during night. Enemy planes moved to new lines near Mount van Barden	
	11		H.Q. decided moved to new lines at Bulloye. Enemy planes over during night	

Army Form C. 2118.

WAR DIARY
or
INTELLIGENCE SUMMARY.
(Erase heading not required.)

H. Wolvers H 15/9/17 to 30/9/17

47" D.A.C

Place	Date	Hour	Summary of Events and Information	Remarks and references to Appendices
MOUNT NOIR	13		2/Lt H.S. Foster, 2/Lt L. Willett posted to 235" Brigade	
	14		60 OR's under 2/Lt Marshall to 7" DA Reserve Park	
	16		one man wounded and animals killed & wounded on ammn fatigue	
			B.O. inspected ammn wagons at echelon	
	17		Lt Ballantyne reporter from Hospital. 20 Reinforcements sent to 235 Bger	
			35 Reinforcement from base. 10 temporary	
	18		S.A.A. Detachment under Captain Mahoney reported	
			to 236" Bde. B.G.R.A. inspected A Echelon lines	
	19		G.O. inspected wagon in B echelon	
	20		2/Lt B.F. Cook, J.H. Austin joined from base	
	22		Lt G.E. Illingworth attached to 235" Bde wounded	
	26		B echelon moved to new lines at N 9 c 9.5.	
			Captain R.S. Moses reported to resume left W.S.E. Illingworth to	
	27, 28, 29		hostile planes over lock night many bombs dropped	
	30		Column moved to Roye horse ambug 3/ on	
			M.g.ham Acapt 47 D.A.C.	

Vol. I. 1 - 8. Oct. 17 inclusive

Army Form C. 2118.

WAR DIARY 47th D.A.C.

or

~~INTELLIGENCE SUMMARY.~~

(Erase heading not required.)

Instructions regarding War Diaries and Intelligence Summaries are contained in F.S. Regs., Part II. and the Staff Manual respectively. Title pages will be prepared in manuscript.

Place	Date	Hour	Summary of Events and Information	Remarks and references to Appendices
Rouge Croix	Octbr 17 1	10.40 A.M.	Hdqrts left Rouge Croix, near Calonne. Marched to BOESINGHEM arriving 4 p.m.	
BOESINGHEM	2	7.30 A.M.	Left BOESINGHEM 7.30 A.M. arrived MARLES-LES-MINES 2 p.m.	
	3		Column left MARLES-LES-MINES 9 A.M. arrived SAVY at 2.45 p.m. Capt. Coates reported from leave. Orders attached HQ R.A. 2nd Lieut. Pearson went forward to take over French the gun from 63rd D.A.C. 2nd Lieut. Hunter attached 236 Bde. R.F.A. 2nd Lieut. Prothero went to hospital sick. 50 reinforcements arrived.	
	4		Column left Savy at 9.30 A.M. and went to ANZIN, taking over Ammn Camp etc from 63 D.A.C. at Anzin. (Reference Sheet 57 B. 1/40000 France) G.O.C. Capt. Gretaninaluckis went in Temp.	
ANZIN	5		Capt. Gough attached 236 Bde R.F.A. Lieut 920293 B.S.M. reported from 235 Bde R.F.A. Pioneer Jouaux (Interpretor) went to French Division	
"	6		Bg. R.A rented lines.	
"	7		Water time came into force.	
"	8		Press representative visited lines. 2nd Lt. G.F. Seaton posted A/235 Battery. 2nd Lieut A.S. Orcutt sent in charge of I.2. Sub-section to work with batteries	

T2134. Wt. W708-776. 500000. 4/15. Sir J. C. & S.

Army Form C. 2118.

WAR DIARY
or
INTELLIGENCE SUMMARY
(Erase heading not required.)

Vol I. 9 – 16.10.17 inclusive

47 DH

Instructions regarding War Diaries and Intelligence Summaries are contained in F.S. Regs., Part II. and the Staff Manual respectively. Title pages will be prepared in manuscript.

Place	Date	Hour	Summary of Events and Information	Remarks and references to Appendices
ANZIN ST. AUBIN	9		T/a/M RSM. W. CAVANNAGH reported to Capt. Stafford R.A.M.C. rejoined from leave. Capt. R.S. Lloyd R.A.M.C. returned to 6th Field Amb. Lieut. McNeill sent up station in charge of 150 head animals conveying bomb this etc while instructor of E. Special Co. R.E. Lieut H. Bowditch posted from B/236 by and attached XIII Corps Counter Battery Office. 2nd Lieut. H.J. Glover attached 236 Bde RFA posted to A/236. Battery. 2nd Lieut W.E. Lawson attached 236 Bde posted to B/236. Battery. 2nd Lieut H.O. Prothero went to hospital.	
"	10		2nd Lieut F.O. Steward attached 235 Bde RFA posted to D/235 Batty. 2/Lt H.S. 1st Army infantry animals attacked at 9.30 AM Lieut Cole H.B. Allen r/Capt. R.A. Gore went to Tent, Bomb, the send up tent or so had arrived.	
"	11		B.G.R.A visited camp about 11.A.M.	
"	12		2nd Lt. Prothero to hospital sick	
"	14		Lieut C.E.H. LLOYD and 27 reinforcements joined from Base.	
"	15		2nd Lieut J.J. Marriage and M.O.R. Wood to T.M. Course. Capt. Gentensradenter rejoined from leave. 15 reinforcements joined. Lieut.	
"	16		J.G. Barron posted to H.Q. R.A. Lieut. McNeill began work as Gas Anti Salvage Officer.	

T 1134. Wt. W708-776. 500000. 4/15. Sir J.C. & S.

Army Form C. 2118.

Vol III. 17-21.10.17. inclusive.

47. DAC

WAR DIARY
or
INTELLIGENCE SUMMARY.
(Erase heading not required.)

Instructions regarding War Diaries and Intelligence Summaries are contained in F. S. Regs., Part II. and the Staff Manual respectively. Title pages will be prepared in manuscript.

Place	Date	Hour	Summary of Events and Information	Remarks and references to Appendices
ANZIN ST. AUBIN	17.		ADCs, Corps inspected animals at 10.0 AM. 2nd Lieut. H.S. Orcutt attached to T.M. Battery. 2nd Lieut. W.R. Stillar went to A'Ground Horse Transport Depot at ABBEVILLE with Surplus vehicles – 16 G.S. wagons and 1 Puellin Cart – Reorganisation of the Column carried out. Surplus personnel – 13 O.R. Despatched to Base. A.D.M.S., Div. visited lines in afternoon. Lieut. W.S.D. Marshall went on leave (18-20). 2nd Lieut H BRAGG and RFA Special Reserve and 2nd Lieut S.H. RENVOIZE esp RFA (TF) reported.	
	18.		"Army Orchestra in Catering" visited Column	
	19.		Major Gen. L KERNAN, United States Army, with B.G. R.A. inspected lines at 2 pm. Capt. Rogers, A.V.C. went on leave.	
	20.		Award of Military Medal to Intelphile Germann notified by Corps R.O. XIII Corps 20.10.47 9/ 20.10.17. London Gazette 9/ 20.10.17 notifies promotion to Lieutenant of 2nd Lieut. Preemy (now appointment of Lieut. Bowditch to be acting Captain (4.9.17).	
	21		2nd Lieut. R.J.H. Pumay returned from leave having been granted an extension to 20.10.17.	

Army Form C. 2118.

Vol II 22-27.10.17 inclusive   47. D.A.C.

WAR DIARY
INTELLIGENCE SUMMARY.
(Erase heading not required.)

Instructions regarding War Diaries and Intelligence
Summaries are contained in F.S. Regs., Part II.
and the Staff Manual respectively. Title pages
will be prepared in manuscript.

Place	Date	Hour	Summary of Events and Information	Remarks and references to Appendices
ANZIN ST AUBIN	22		2nd Lieut. H.O. Prothero rejoined from hospital. Lieut Col H.B. Allen rejoined from leave. 2nd Lieut W.G.B. Thompson rejoined from England. Captain Lord granted extension of leave by W.O. to 6.11.17.	
	23.		Lieut-Col. H.B. Allen attached to 235 Brigade R.F.A to command Right group. Special fatigue ("burying party") of 1 Lieut + 1 Serjeant, 3 N.C.O. and 30 men up the line GGR, 1st Army Infantry Surplus animals at 3 pm B.G. R.A. rides. Lines about 3 pm.	
	24.		2nd Lieut H Rogers Bragg attached 235. Bde. R.F.A. Captain brooks (attached 236. Bde R.F.A.) and Capt. Hodgkinson went on leave (24th Oct to 6th Nov). Lieut Lloyd and 2nd Lieut Ramage attached 236 Bde R.F.A. Special fatigue under 2nd Lt Army as on 23rd inst.	
	25.		Party went to Gibraltar on 17th inst rejoined except 2nd Lieut Spillers. 2nd Lieut G.P. Hawkins went on leave (26.Oct to 5th Nov).	
	26.		2nd Lieut Spillers rejoined from Gibraltar.	
	27		2nd Lieut Spillers attached 235 Brigade R.F.A. Notification in Bng Part II Orders of telegram by W.O. of 12.10.17 of leave granted to 2nd Lieut Garnett	

Army Form C. 2118.

WAR DIARY
or
INTELLIGENCE SUMMARY.
(Erase heading not required.)

Vol V 28-31.10.17 inclusive 47th D.A.C.

Instructions regarding War Diaries and Intelligence Summaries are contained in F. S. Regs, Part II. and the Staff Manual respectively. Title pages will be prepared in manuscript.

Place	Date	Hour	Summary of Events and Information	Remarks and references to Appendices
MAZIN ST AUBIN	28		Lieut A.W. WHITTET and 2nd Lieut Y. LIMERICK reported and O.R.s rejoined from T.M. Course. 2nd Lieut J.H. McDonald from X/47 T.M. Battery and Lieut P.S. Leyne from 235 Bde R.F.A. posted to 9 Bde.	
	29		R.S.M. Cavanagh to hospital. Special future G ("turkey trotting") under Lieut Thompson. Lieut W.S.S. Marshall rejoined from leave.	
	30		2nd Lt. J.J. Ramage posted to X/47 Battery (T.M.) as from 29th inst - reported. 2nd Lieut B.F. Paul and 6.O.R. to Mobeny T.M. School	
	31		Capt. R. Boyles A.V.C. rejoined from leave. Lieut. W.S.S. Marshall and 5.O.R. went to Abbeville on Veterinary Course at No 14. Vety Hosp.	

Hilton Warburg Capt
Lt. Colonel Comm[?]
47. Divisional AMM. Column T.F.

Volume I 1/11/17 to 14/4/17

Army Form C. 2118.

WAR DIARY
or
INTELLIGENCE SUMMARY.
(Erase heading not required.)

47 D.A.C.

Hour, Date, Place	Summary of Events and Information	Remarks and references to Appendices
ANZIN		
now ARRAS		
1/11/17	Capt S.E. Furley joined from Base, posted to Command SAA Section	
	B.G.R.A visited lines at 3 p.m. D.D.R. 1st army visited lines	
2/11/17	R.O. inspected Section Animals for the Dir'l Competition	
4/11/17	C.O. inspected Section Turnouts for the Div'l Competition. No 2 Section selected	
	to represent Column	
5/11/17	4th A. Farry proceeded on leave	
6/11/17	Captains A.A. Wintle + W. Hodgkinson + W.D. Hawkins rejoined from leave	
7/11/17	M.G.R.A 1st Army inspected lines 2.30 p.m.	
8/11/17	Lt. Col. A.B. Allen attd 235 Brigade proceeded to England for course at	
	Shoeburyness. G.O.C. Division inspected lines.	
9/11/17	Capt C.W. Egerton evacuated to G.H.Q. Italy.	
12/11/17	13 men paraded for selection as Shoemakers. 3 selected.	
13/11/17	Lt Marshall, 5 O.R's rejoined from Vet. Course.	
14/11/17	14 O.R's proceeded to 1st army T.M School.	

Volume II. 16/11/17 to 27/11/17.

Army Form C. 2118.

WAR DIARY
or
INTELLIGENCE SUMMARY.   47 D.A.C.

(Erase heading not required.)

Hour, Date, Place	Summary of Events and Information	Remarks and references to Appendices
AMYIN. 16th	Lt. W.S.D. Marshall proceeded with 33 ors to collect remounts for B.A.C.	
17th	Capt. P.A Lowe medically boarded and struck off strength 9/11/17.	
18th	Sections practised entraining of horses & vehicles.	
20th	Capt. Cooke rejoined from D.A. Capt. S.E. Pixley attd to 4. D.A.	
21st	The 47 DAC moved to OHLAIN. Lt. Marshall rejoined from remount collecting.	
22nd	Lt. A. Farm rejoined from leave.	
OHLAIN. 23rd	The 47 DAC moved to WANQUETIN.	
WANQUETIN 24th	" " " . SAPIGNES.	
SAPIGNES 25th	" " " . BUS.	
BUS		
VALLULART 27th	" " " . VALLULART WOOD this area a suspected WOOD	
	move, the column moving from their camp with 1 hour of the order being given.	

Volume III 27/11/17

WAR DIARY
or
INTELLIGENCE SUMMARY

(Erase heading not required.)

Army Form C. 2118.

47 D.A.C.

Hour, Date, Place	Summary of Events and Information	Remarks and references to Appendices
VALLULART WOOD		
27th	Lt Col H.S. Allin rejoined from course in England.	
28th	RSM S.G. Dransfield assumed duties of RSM. RSM A.E. Wright transferred to A/236th D.A.	
29th	2Lt.s J. Boyd, R.H. Smith joined from England.	
30th	S.A.A. Section moved to Metz relieving SAA Section 62nd DAC. Heavy German attack our line pierced in places 235th Bde ordered into action in the open.	

Meyler
Adjt 47th DAC
for S.O.
Commd 47

Volume I 1/11/17 R.E.
15/12/17

47th D.A.C.   Army Form C. 2118.

WAR DIARY
or
INTELLIGENCE SUMMARY.
(Erase heading not required.)

Hour, Date, Place	Summary of Events and Information	Remarks and references to Appendices
VALLULART WOOD Dec 15	Major S.E. Crosby reported from D.A.	
2—	J.E.P.S. Lyne posted to B/236 Bty	
3	L/C.R.A. Dodgson + 2 W/Cs. J/C-S.J. Stepford posted from [illeg]	
4/45	Q.R. book to Major	
5/45	S.A. Baty service from here. S.A.A. etc [illeg]	
	Many horse suffering from battle please [illeg] my op [illeg]	
6	Horse [illeg] vaccined 5-15 P.M. Buck Supper	
9	Column moved to new line at Bus	
10	J.P.S. Lyne, W.C. Brown reported sick. L/C.M.J.T. Wait for [illeg]	
	posted to 1st Portugu. Rest for Artly.	
12	L/C S.R. Dodgson posted to C/235. 2/L/50 Buckeff. R. Jolimore	
	returns from leave. June [illeg] struck off strength now from 62 D.A.C.	
14	B.G.S. Wagar Stan attached to + 3rd Nov H.A.H.A.C.	
15	J.E. P.S. Lyne reported to B/236.	

B.U.S.

WAR DIARY
or
INTELLIGENCE SUMMARY.

Army Form C. 2118.

Nelson II 16/9/17
47-DAC
31/1-7/17

(Erase heading not required.)

Instructions regarding War Diaries and Intelligence Summaries are contained in F.S. Regs., Part II and the Staff Manual respectively. Title pages will be prepared in manuscript.

Hour, Date, Place	Summary of Events and Information	Remarks and references to Appendices
BUS 16	Lt A Bonechek att'd to N 53 Bg received Dist	No 1 & 2 Section
	made trip for 235 Bde wagon line Lt/Bg to 47 C	left on 4th Sept
	N Harvey with Lt/Bg to new camp. Did march to BUS.	
	Lieut Col Hewin MO overseer hospital for visit.	
17	Lt F J Bellamy joined & posted to M/R Section Yes	
	B F Land att'd to L 33-B'de Lieut M I Malon oc 236 B'de	
22	Capt G R Kimberly Lieuts C/233-B's	
23	W.O. J Dunkin attd 233-B'de motorcar	
26	Pte Julian injured	
28	Capt A L Elliot proceed'd on leave	Hep Supernum Officer to YPRES
29	Lieut O C Batty to 236 B'de 2 IC	
30	Lieut G A Gerrard to III et Inf Gp adm	

Macfarlane Lt/Cel
47 DAC

Army Form C. 2118.

WAR DIARY
or
INTELLIGENCE SUMMARY.
(Erase heading not required.)

Instructions regarding War Diaries and Intelligence Summaries are contained in F. S. Regs., Part II. and the Staff Manual respectively. Title pages will be prepared in manuscript.

47th D.A.C.

Place	Date	Hour	Summary of Events and Information	Remarks and references to Appendices
BUS	2		Lt. J.S. Ballantyne reported for duty. Capt. & M. & Mck hammer 1/4/16	
	3		Lt. J.S. Ballantyne & 2/Lt. A. Leary & 4 NCOs to Graham Leavy Bus Depot	
			Course during attendance. Duty billets [illegible] of Lt wounded	
	5		2/Lt. W.H. Ramage attd 463 Bn. Jr. T.M. Btys report out.	
	6		2/15 2/Lt. J.J. Patterson & Swishs attd 3rd Army T.M. Mess	
			Capt. R. & Bryson and 4 O.Rs. reported 1st O.K.	
	7		Lt. J.J. Merrich reported for duty. Lieut. Johnson went to hospital	
			at Bernancourt having the following takin. Deep ship work	
			37 GS Wagons 12 LGS Wagons about mk each of 30 mules	
			H.P.Q.M.J. Henry sent over SAA Depot from 17th Divl D.A.C. to 47th Divl D.A.C.	
			Lt. Col. D. Marsh. Howard having tempy command D.A.C. during absence	
DERNANCOURT	8		Column moved to St. Gratien	
S. GRATIEN	9		Capt. W.G. Loch proceeded on leave, 47th Divl Q for attendance	
"	10		2/Lt. J.J. Blackburn proceed on leave	
PONT NOYELLES	12		Column moved to PONT NOYELLES	
	13		Capt. H.H. Collack rejoined from leave. B&RA medical exam	

Army Form C. 2118.

WAR DIARY
or
INTELLIGENCE SUMMARY

(Erase heading not required.)

Instructions regarding War Diaries and Intelligence Summaries are contained in F.S. Regs., Part II. and the Staff Manual respectively. Title pages will be prepared in manuscript.

Army Form C. 2118.

Name: November 14/11/16   47th D.A.C.

Pages: 31/11/16

Place	Date	Hour	Summary of Events and Information	Remarks and references to Appendices
PONT NOYELLES	14		2nd Lt W.H. Vivian returned from Lybia	
	15		Mr J.J. Blackburn & 19 O.Rs proceeded to Albert to collect ammunition	
	16		Lt Col A.B. Allen to take command of left group during absence of Lt Col Bearsley on leave	
	17		37 L.D. horses + mules were sent to remounts	
	18		Major M.J. Bates rejoined	
	20		2nd Lt G.W. Rowland returned to duty	
	22		2nd Lt E.J. Reed & 1 N.C.O. & 10 D & 10. Ser. men to D.A.C.s on being over-establishment on reform	
	23		Mr E.J.G. Blackburn & 6 Batteries from 3rd Army T.M. Bk.	
			B.S.M. Blenchion to England on leave. Officer over strength.	
			Mr G.O. Day returned from leave	
	25		Mr S. Parry & 2 N.C.Os returned from Inf. School Course	
	26		2nd Lt W.E. Champion posted 233 Bde 1st Lt A.G.G. Appleton to 1st T.M. 2nd Lt G.G. Ramsey to 236 Bde	
	28		1st Relief Party to Bar-	
	29		2nd Lt Robin adde 235 Bde	
	31		1st Relieve Party rejoined	
			B.G.R.A. inspected the lines	

Montgomerie Capt
a/Adjt 47th D.A.C.

WAR DIARY or INTELLIGENCE SUMMARY

Army Form C. 2118.

From 1/2/18 to 16/2/18

47th - D.A.C.

Place	Date	Hour	Summary of Events and Information	Remarks and references to Appendices
PONT NOYELLES	1		Capt Watts proceeded on leave	
	2		2/Lt R.B. Tatman & J. Blackburn & D. Day to 3rd Army Arty School	
	3		Capt A.J. Snowden M.C. R.A.M.C. reptd from 1st London Off. Centre for duty as M.O.	
	4		Lt Col Tumer M.D.R.C. U.S.A. left to join No 17 Base Hospital B.E.F.	
	5		2/Lt R.M. Smith reported 29 Reinforcements annex	
	6		2/Lt W.J.D. Moulden to D.A. for attachment	
	8		Lt E.C. Ingram proceeded on leave	
	9		Capt M.P. Dickman R.A.M.C.(T) reported to ...	
	11		Relief party proceeded to BUS... 40 O.R's posted to B.Ex	
	12		Capt J.S. Taylor, J.S. Carr, J. Balmright, A. Lethenie, A. Mulherron, reported from leave	
			C.S.M. Mulherron reported to D.T.M.O. for attendance	
	14		2/Lt B.W. Mulherron to attd 235 BDE 2/Lt J. Balmright attd 236 BDE	
	15		D.R.L.S. 47- Div unfit for animals	
	16		Lt J. A. Wright rejoined from leave	

WAR DIARY or **INTELLIGENCE SUMMARY.**
(Erase heading not required.)

Army Form C. 2118.

A/Nelson IV 16/2/15 to /1/A.7th D.A.C. 28/2/15

Place	Date	Hour	Summary of Events and Information	Remarks and references to Appendices
PORT NATAL S.S.	16		2nd Lt L. Elyé reported from leave. Left India reserve from leave.	
	19		Capt Garbutt to 47th D.A.	
	20		2nd Lt J.S. Inglut, 10 O.R.s to 3rd Army T.M. School	
	21		Lt Col J.B. Allen reported/proceeded on leave	
	22		Capt J MacBride A.V.C. reported for duty	
	23		Remainder of personnel at D.A.C. Havre sent to 17th D.A.	
			Augmentation of S.A.T. Depot handed over to 17th D.A.	
	24		Capt A. Brydon & W.L. Hopkins Geer, 24 Lt Col Rogers	
			H. Buchanan departed.	
			½ D. Mule to S.A.T. Depot handed over to 65th Div.	
			Tweasith 2nd Lt G.B. Ingram reported from leave	
	25		2nd Lt G.C. Ingram reported in Column.	
	27		2nd Lt F. Bullock/Lyon reported with 136 Indians from Base Depot.	
			B.S.M. Moss & 5 Gunners posted to No 1 Section	
	28		2nd Lt E. Green reported, posted to No 1 Section.	

Maj/. Ing 47th D.A.C.

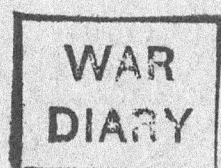

47th DIVISIONAL AMMUNITION COLUMN, R.F.A.

M A R C H

1 9 1 8

WAR DIARY
or
INTELLIGENCE SUMMARY.
(Erase heading not required.)

Army Form C. 2118.

47th D.A.C.

March 1918

WO 34

Place	Date	Hour	Summary of Events and Information	Remarks and references to Appendices
PONT NOYELLES	1		Remainder of John Section regained from Base with D.A.	
	2		Capt W.J. Crooks regained from D.A.	
	3		2nd Lt M.B. Allen proceeded on leave. 2nd Lt A.J. Hammond joined from Base	
	4		2nd Lt A. Marsh attd 235 Bde, 2nd Lt A. Hallman from T.M.B.	
DERNANCOURT	5		Column moved from Pont Noyelles to Dernancourt.	
	6		2nd Lt L.A. Green attd 235th Bde, 2nd Lt J.D. Day, R. Johnson attd 236th Bde, 2nd Lt C.W. Cowan proceeded to 5th ??? of 5th ??? of the Indian ??? Army	
			No more on R.L.C. 3rd Jan?	
	8		Lt W.H.F.J. Meeny proceeded on leave	
	9		2nd Lt J.J. Lloyd regained from T.M. Bde, 2nd Lt X 47th TM By	
	12		2nd Lt D.L. Bradshaw proceed to join 126 D.F.D. Bde. Suffering from ???	
			of wound from ???	
	13		Capt. W.H.F.J. Metcalf joined 19 Regiments arrived	
	14		2nd Lt A. Shepherd joined	
	15		2nd Lt A. Long proceed on leave	
	16		11 Other mks Reinforcements arrived, 2nd Lt J. Allen upholds from R.A.F.A. Bde	

Army Form C. 2118.

Volume II

WAR DIARY
or
INTELLIGENCE SUMMARY.
(Erase heading not required.)

Instructions regarding War Diaries and Intelligence Summaries are contained in F. S. Regs., Part II. and the Staff Manual respectively. Title pages will be prepared in manuscript.

19/3/18 to 23/3/18

47th D.A.C.

Place	Date	Hour	Summary of Events and Information	Remarks and references to Appendices
DERNACOURT	19		Lt. S.B. Ingram proceeded to report to 2nd DA ARP.	
	20		Lt. Col R.B. Allan recovered from leave	
	21"		2/Lt. J. Elliot & A. Duff proceeded on leave. ARP taken over from 2nd DA	
			Very heavy gunfire at night	
	22		SAA section moved to Dernancourt to take over from SAA section 2nd Div	
			2/Lt A.B. Douglas returned from leave	
	23		News received enemy in Dernancourt and that the D.A.C. section had	
			moved another column no news so far as to where it had gone	
	24		The day while I believed I was going there ordered to hear of the	
			village turned over civilians any women the D.A.C. &	
			Dernancourt left hurriedly Villagers began to leave the village	
			with their effects What I could tell was our	
			own wounded, women and covered horses	
6 mars	25		Gun fire perceptibly nearer by the our officers and	
			own men and enemy drawn in Bazentin the Ridge	
			At 2 a.m. D.O. gave orders for the column to be	

WAR DIARY or INTELLIGENCE SUMMARY

Army Form C. 2118.

Volume VII 25/3/16 to 47th D.A.C.
Title pages 26/3/16

Place	Date	Hour	Summary of Events and Information	Remarks and references to Appendices
On the march	25		recd. by the main body. I am at 7 am orders were given by the V.L.G. D.A.Cs. for the column to march to cover the PUISIEUX AU MONT area. The information available showed that at SERRE & the German and the enemy had to [illegible] been about one mile east of MAILLY MAILLET evening. There about 4.30 p.m. at 7 p.m. [illegible] orders [illegible] were given by a staff officer to move to FONQUEVILLERS [illegible] march off at 6 p.m. and an instruction until 2 a.m. [illegible] at all events be in [illegible] traffic at one [illegible] during [illegible] half 500 [illegible] [illegible] on [illegible] side when [illegible] [illegible] and but very [illegible] [illegible] as they were made to wait	
FONQUEVILLERS	26		On the 26th the [illegible] [illegible] could over the [illegible] of SOUASTRE about 10 guns were in the direction of SOUASTRE off about 10 AM while [illegible] were [illegible] column moved off FONQUEVILLERS and SOUASTRE German [illegible] as British staff officers [illegible] [illegible] the [illegible] on [illegible] by enemy the	

WAR DIARY or INTELLIGENCE SUMMARY

Army Form C. 2118.

Volume IV 20/3/16   47= D.A.C.
Title pages 30/3/16

Place	Date	Hour	Summary of Events and Information	Remarks and references to Appendices
GAUDIEMPRÉ	26		Back loading and thought not to be heard on for several days. Our amm: cartain amount of thousand horses harness there.	
			GAUDIEMPRÉ gullery in hand with 235 & Bde up, also with 233 & Bde	
			May, Greenhorn called ... heavy thought... attached to 62= D.A.	
	27		Major ... to March to hospital sick	
	28		School with 236= Bde at HANNESCAMPS. 74= A/g Ammn and 15 DR's handed in. 62= ARP at Lucheral.	
SOUASTRE	29		Moved at 10 a.m. to new area at SOUASTRE. Sent T Bn A/g Noi but up 47 & Div.	
			assumed command of 47 & Div. located at HENCU thence had heard of Brch with supply column from dump.	
	30		SAA lorries parked at HERISSART. Major A Murray reports for duty 74= Bhyr Amnn from Base	

May [signature] Major 47 DAC

WAR DIARY or INTELLIGENCE SUMMARY

Army Form C. 2118.

of A.R.P. 47th D. Bn
Army not shown

Place	Date	Hour	Summary of Events and Information	Remarks and references to Appendices
Equancourt	21/3/18		Orders to take over Dumps cancelled. Dump Staff arrived at about 7.0PM	
	22.3.18	10.0AM	Gun Ammunition & Infantry Dumps taken over from 2nd D.A.C.	
		5.0PM	Orders received to report at 47th D.A. Acting under instructions from D.A.Q.M.G. & Staff Capt., I proceeded to LE MESNIL & selected sites for new dumps. Returning to H.Q. & proceeded with O.C. S.A.A. Section to ETRICOURT to arrange removal of ammunition from FINS Dump to LE MESNIL. Owing to the proximity of the enemy this could not be carried out.	
		9.30PM	Orders received to withdraw personnel from METZ Dump. Ben Carts sent out to carry out this order. He failed to reach Dump & did not return. FINS Dump evacuated.	
LE MESNIL	23.3.18	3.30AM	Acting under orders from 47 D.A. proceeded with Dump Staff to LE MESNIL. Small S.A.A Dump formed on ROCQUIGNY Road. Gun Ammunition asked for by Light Railway did not arrive.	
		2.0PM	Orders received to proceed to LE TRANSLOY Dump	
LE TRANSLOY		6.0PM	LE TRANSLOY Dump taken over in conjunction with 63rd Div.	

Volume II

WAR DIARY of A.R.P. 47th D.A.C. during the withdrawal
or
INTELLIGENCE SUMMARY.
(Erase heading not required.)

Army Form C. 2118.

Instructions regarding War Diaries and Intelligence Summaries are contained in F.S. Regs., Part II. 24/3/18 and the Staff Manual respectively. Title pages 26/3/18 will be prepared in manuscript.

Place	Date	Hour	Summary of Events and Information	Remarks and references to Appendices
E. TRANSLOY	24.3.18	8.0 AM	Orders received by phone from b.ofo to evacuate Dump & proceed to LONGUEVAL & report to 47th D.A. H.Q., thence to TRONES WOOD. Small dump of ammunition found, which were hit by enemy shell-fire shortly afterwards.	
LONGUEVAL		2.0 PM		
TRONES WOOD				
CONTALMAISON		3.30 PM	Proceeded to HQ 47 DA at CONTALMAISON, where orders were received to go to POZIERES Dump.	
POZIERES		8.0 PM	POZIERES Dump taken over	
	25.4.18	10.0 AM	POZIERES Dump evacuated leaving small quantity of ammunition. Ordered to proceed to MEAULTE Dump	
MEAULTE		12 noon	Arrived MEAULTE Dump & assisted V.B. of Dump Staff.	
		10.30 PM	Took over Dump	
	26.4.18	8.30 AM	Received orders to evacuate Dump & proceed to MAILLY-MAILLET	
SENLIS		12 noon	Reported to HQ 47 DA en route, at SENLIS. Orders to proceed to MAILLY-MAILLET cancelled & instructions received to report to O.C. SAA Section at VAUCHELLES.	
VAUCHELLES		4.0 PM	Joined SAA Section at VAUCHELLES.	

F. L. Ingram
Lieut R.F.A.(T)
% 47 ARP

2353 Wt. W2544/1454 700,000 5/15 D.D. & L. A.D.S.S.Forms/C. 2118.

VOLUME I

Instructions regarding War Diaries and Intelligence Summaries are contained in F.S. Regs., Part II. and the Staff Manual respectively. Title pages will be prepared in manuscript.

Army Form C. 2118.

WAR DIARY
or
INTELLIGENCE SUMMARY

S.A.A. Section
22.3.18 to 30/3/18.

47 = D A C

(Erase heading not required.)

Place	Date	Hour	Summary of Events and Information	Remarks and references to Appendices
DERNANCOURT	22/3/18		S.A.A. Section moved to ETRICOURT arrived at 6pm. Heavily shelled on route. 12 wagons detailed to remove dump. Owing to proximity of enemy this was not possible. Section ordered to withdraw all mules & wagons at once. Moved to SAILLY-SAILLISEL-COMBLES road	
	23/3/18		Arriving at 4am. Enemy shelling became considerable. Camped by roadside. Moved to Le Mesnil 10am arriving at 12 noon. Left Le MESNIL 4pm for ROCQUIGNY. Left ROCQUIGNY 6.30pm moved to SAILLY-SAILLISEL - Combles Road. Enemy shelling heavily.	
	24.3.18.		Left SAILLY-SAILLISEL 1am & proceeded to Butte de Warlencourt. Proceeding Bapaume road being used as reserve line. Arrived shelled. Arrived Butte de Warlencourt 12 noon left there 4.30 pm for Longueval on road. Bombed & shelled by enemy aircraft. Left enemy occupied Longueval so retired course to MILLENCOURT.	
	25/3/18		Arrived MILLENCOURT 4am. Bombed presently through ALBERT. No casualties. Left MILLENCOURT 8am for BOUZINCOURT owing to enemy shelled BOUZINCOURT 4pm order received to	

Army Form C. 2118.

S.A.A Section
47 - D.A.C

WAR DIARY
or
INTELLIGENCE SUMMARY.
(Erase heading not required.)

Instructions regarding War Diaries and Intelligence Summaries are contained in F. S. Regs., Part II. and the Staff Manual respectively. Title pages will be prepared in manuscript.

Place	Date	Hour	Summary of Events and Information	Remarks and references to Appendices
	25/3/18		Withdrew left BOUZINCOURT 5 p.m for VAUCHELLES arriving at 10.30 p.m	
	26/3/18		Left VAUCHELLES for PUCHEVILLERS arriving at 10.30 a.m	
	29/3/18		Section moved to HERISSART.	
	31/3/18		Still at HERISSART	

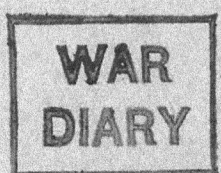

47th DIVISIONAL AMMUNITION COLUMN.

A P R I L

1 9 1 8

Army Form C. 2118.

WAR DIARY
or
INTELLIGENCE SUMMARY.
(Erase heading not required.)

Army Form 2/4/18 to
47th D.A.C.
13-1/4/18

WO 95

Instructions regarding War Diaries and Intelligence Summaries are contained in F.S. Regs., Part II. and the Staff Manual respectively. Title pages will be prepared in manuscript.

Place	Date	Hour	Summary of Events and Information	Remarks and references to Appendices
GOUIN	2		Column moved from Souastre to Souain	
	3		Lt. Col. C.A. Bates proceeded to B/236 Bty	
	4		Lt. Col. H. H. J. Lang completed tour	
	5		Inspected Longuevan for 47th & 235th Bdes	
	6	2nd	Lt. Roug returned from leave. 2nd Lt. McKenna returned from leave	
			and 2nd Lt. Offany in a horse garage	
	7	7.20	Reinforcements sent to 233rd Bde. Lt. N.B. Black reported as attd	
		23.6	6th Bde	
	8		Capt. W.J. Rankin reported to DA	
	9	4.2	ORS joined from leave 2 reinforcements to 235th Bde 29 to 236th Bde	
	11	5.AA	Section moved to HAVERNAS. Enemy planes over between 8-9pm	
			a few bombs dropped	
	12	5.AA	Section to DOMQUEUR. 2nd Lt. O.R. Smith to attn 236th Bde	
		7.45	D.D. Davis J.D. Lang attd 235th Bde H.H. Brackett to 33rd DA	
	13	5.AA	Section to CUMONVILLE. 47th DA commanding of 37th DA	
	14	2nd	Lt C Wheeler joined from 233rd Bde	
	15	20	reinforcements arrived from PUCHEVILLERS. 2nd Lt W. Mackown posted to No 1 Section	

WAR DIARY
or
INTELLIGENCE SUMMARY.

(Erase heading not required.)

Army Form C. 2118.

Volume IV 1/3/15 to 30/3/15

47th = D.A.C.

Instructions regarding War Diaries and Intelligence Summaries are contained in F.S. Regs., Part II. and the Staff Manual respectively. Title pages will be prepared in manuscript.

Place	Date	Hour	Summary of Events and Information	Remarks and references to Appendices
COUIN	16		Same under orders of 42nd D.A.	
	19		Formed up a few H.Y. ammunition to 47th D.A.C.	
	20		Lt. C. Stammers posted from 42nd D.A.	
	21		No Hope flares reported and posted to Wolchehn. Edward Manegre	
	22		25 Reinforcements for D.A. arrived being given to receive the horses	
	23		26 Mule convoys to arrive	
	24		Lt. Stammers to S.A.A. Same under orders of 2 New Zealand D.A.	
	25		19 reinforcements arrive	
	27		Lt. J.E.F. Miller reported 15 reinforcements to the Base	
	28		Lt. Col. L.B. Allen to F.A. with Capt. Banks. reinforced S.A.A.	
	29		S.A.A. India moves forward	
	30		Lt. M.J. Black to 236t Base for attachment	

Macfarlane Capt.
47th DAC.

WAR DIARY or INTELLIGENCE SUMMARY

Army Form C. 2118.

47th D.A.C.

1/5/18 to 12/5/18

Place	Date	Hour	Summary of Events and Information	Remarks and references to Appendices
COUIN	1		2d/Lt A. Falconer to X 47th T.M. Batt.	
	2		2d/Lt A. Falconer rejoined from X 47th T.M.	
	3		DTMO and TM Bgd. arrived	
	4		2d/Lt A.G.F. Miller attd to A 236 Bde. 2d/Lt A Falconer joined X 47 T.M. B 35	
	5		SAA section moved to BEAUCOURT	
	6		Lt L.B. Inman to England to report to War Office. ARP handed over to	
			TM Bde. moved to Beaucourt	
	41st D.A.			
GEZAINCOURT	7		Column less SAA Section moved to GEZAINCOURT. 61 Reinforcements arrived	
			2d/Lt J. Milne to hospital	The R.A.F.
ST OUEN	8		Column less SAA moved to ST OUEN. 2d/Lt V Laurenich & Inglis to Farnborough	
BRAY-LES-MAREUIL	9		Column less SAA moved to BRAY-LES-MAREUIL	
	10		2d/Lt H.E. Green rejoined. Major Malcolm att'd from 47th D.A.	
	11		Lt Col A.H. Browning actg BGRA morphine horse	
	12		2d/Lt L.B. Wells, 2d/Lt A. Walker, L. Tindley and 2d/Lt R.W. Mallett and	
			W.W. Baker reported as reinforcements	

Army Form C. 2118.

WAR DIARY
or
INTELLIGENCE SUMMARY.
(Erase heading not required.)

47 - D.A.C.

Volume II 13/5/18 to 29/5/18

Place	Date	Hour	Summary of Events and Information	Remarks and references to Appendices
BRAY-LES-MAREUIL	15		Lt W.S.D. Marshall proceeded to 47th Div R.F.A. Leave Staff Leave.	
	16		Lt. F. Shoemaker to F.A. Scats	
	17		DDR 3rd Army inspection annexed. BGRA and MBM arrived and stayed the night	
	18		BGRA inspection Echelons in full marching order. Spec MG lab	
			No 3rd Echelon gun instruction	
	20		Major General Beauvoir R.A. 4th Army visited the lines	
	21		Lt. M.L.E. Robinson posted from 103 A.F.A. Bde to 233rd Bde	
			Column less S.A.A. Section to Bourdon BOURDON	
BOURDON	22		Column moved HQs to BEAUCOURT	
BEAUCOURT	23			
	24		Capt W.S. Lake rejoins from 3rd Echelon and assumes in Command	
	25		A.R.P. lobes on at C.11-a-6-6. Lt Ingram in charge	
	26		Lt Hammersh to A.R.P. Lt F.J. Ballantyne attd 47th DA	
			Lt A.J. Snow Joined from Base 27-18 F.J. Milling joined for F.A.	
	29		Lt G. Whitley Hart on duty at lats horses. Depot own Renouvelle	
			Lt. L.L. Chandler joined from Base	

WAR DIARY
or
INTELLIGENCE SUMMARY

(Erase heading not required.)

Army Form C. 2118.

47 = D.A.C.

29/5/15 to
3/5/15

Place	Date	Hour	Summary of Events and Information	Remarks and references to Appendices
BEAUCOURT	30		2/Lt. E Edwards, B.5 Group reported from here Nothing unusual	
			active during night	
	31		Every little active in level area 24 beep wounds to T.M.S	
			16 det forward is to D/233 R Bty Lt. W.S.D. Moulton agreed from	
			47". R.	

W. Johnson Lt
Capt 47 D.A.C.

Army Form C. 2118.

No. 1.   47D Am Col

WAR DIARY
or
INTELLIGENCE SUMMARY.
(Erase heading not required.)

1/6/18
to
9/6/18

Vol 37

Instructions regarding War Diaries and Intelligence Summaries are contained in F. S. Regs., Part II. and the Staff Manual respectively. Title pages will be prepared in manuscript.

Place	Date	Hour	Summary of Events and Information	Remarks and references to Appendices
BEAUCOURT	1/6/18		Cattle shewing in Village 7 A.M. Lieut. N.S. Gorton to 47 D.A. 30 Reing. movement to Boyne.	
			Enemy fired about 30 rounds Gas Shell in and around BEAUCOURT.	
	2/6/18		If England regained from hospital. S.A.A. dump at Contay handed over to 18th Division.	
	--		Dump at C.3. Centre (Maj B2D now) taken over from 58 Division.	
	--		Capt. N.S. Gorton appointed Staff Captain to 47 D.A.	
	3/6/18		Lieut. F. STANNARD transferred B' at Base.	
	4/6/18		2/Lt G.W. MacKinnon completed 18 months commissioned service. Lt-Gen. Sir E.L. ELLIOT, K.C.B., D.S.O. Indian Army visited Column preparing to proceed to Southern Persia.	
	5/6/18		Lt. W.S.D. MARSHALL left to proceed in lieu to England. Lt 4 to 20 -- 2/Lt H.S. HAMMOND and B.S.M. OLDRIGHT attached to T. MORGAN Battery. 2/Lt E.L. CARDNER to D.R.P. 2/Lt C.V. PERRIN to H.Q. 235 Bde. 2/Lt L. EDYE attached	
	--		Lt A HINDLEY attached D/236 Battery. 2/Lt L. EDMUNDS attached H.Q. 235 Bde. 2/Lt L. EDYE attached D/236 Battery. Major L.S. KEYNER reported.	
	6/6/18		2/Lt F.E. INGHAM joined from Base.	
	7/6/18		2/Lt E.L. CHANDLER left to join 31 D.A. and S.O.S.	
	8/6/18		Major L.S. KEYNER to 235 Bde. R.F.A. Maj B.S. GASCOIGNE left to join 31 D.A. and S.O.S.	
	9/6/18		2/Lt L.S. SANS, A.W. HAYES and W.L. HOPE joined from Base. W.O.1 WILSON Goods killed.	

Army Form C. 2118.

No 2

WAR DIARY
or
~~INTELLIGENCE SUMMARY.~~
(Erase heading not required.)

10/6/18
2/6/18

Instructions regarding War Diaries and Intelligence Summaries are contained in F. S. Regs., Part II. and the Staff Manual respectively. Title pages will be prepared in manuscript.

Place	Date	Hour	Summary of Events and Information	Remarks and references to Appendices
BEAUCOURT	10/6/18		2/Lt W.W. USHER attached 47th T.M. Battery. 2/Lt H.O. BROTHEROE attached 236 Brigade transferred to England sick	
	13/6/18		Lt. Col A.H. BOWRING inspected Lines. Enemy shelled in vicinity of No 2 Section Lines, no casualties reported.	
	14/6/18		2/Lt G.W. MARTINEAU to 47 A.R.P.	
	15/6/18		Lt B.M. DE LAS CASAS attached from R.N.D. Howitzer (Kensington) T.F. Reserve 1/6/18	
	16/6/18		2/Lt J.W. HOWLETT (WOOLLETT?) posted to 5th Corps Gas School from 23rd Corps	
			Lt DE LAS CASAS posted dept to B.E.G. B.Co. R.F.A.	
	17/6/18		No Comrades and 8 Men from 47 D.A. Rank and ratin's Change 2/Lt H.P. EVANS & E. BAIRDON 2nd Lts	
			B. Base Reinmt. dept at DIEPPE as casualties Casualty C.H.G. M. O.B./3/6/5 of 10/6/15 Enemy fired	
			for ½ hrs in vicinity of No 1 Sub Sect R.A. No 1 Column at Lt 2 Sub out.	
	18/6/15		L.C. MESSNER Transferred to 107 B.F.D. Bde R.F.A. (R.A.) Corps No S.S. 27 pure order 5/4/15	
	19/6/15		S.A.A. Dump handed over to 518 Division. Enemy fired reinforcements at very slow rate at 7 H	
			MAC. Point and MORIGNY.	
	20/6/15		R.P. handed over to 105 O. Pdr.. D.A. and Section moved	
			Enemy fired for approx 3/4 hr about 10:30 P.M. in vicinity of H.Q. Lines.	
	21/6/15		S.A.A. Sect moved at 12 hours to BRELLY.	
CONTAY			No 2 Section Lines shelled	

T.J134. Wt. W708—776. 500000. 4/15. Sir J. C. & S.

Army Form C. 2118.

N° 3   22/4/15
        to
        30/4/15

WAR DIARY
or
INTELLIGENCE SUMMARY.
(Erase heading not required.)

Instructions regarding War Diaries and Intelligence Summaries are contained in F. S. Regs., Part II. and the Staff Manual respectively. Title pages will be prepared in manuscript.

Place	Date	Hour	Summary of Events and Information	Remarks and references to Appendices
BEAUCOURT	22/4/15		Colonel Reid C.A.A. Boulton reported to War Littleton again at HQ RFA.	
	23/4/15		2/Lt L.S. Sims attached 47 Div.	
	24/4/15		1/Lt C.L. H. Thompson reported from base. Lt W.S.D. Marshall reported from leave.	
			2/Lt Mockett reported from the base.	
	25/4/15		C.R.A. visited Colonel Rev. S.A.A. Lt A. Hindley attached 236 Bde posted to 30 D.S.C. Curtis	
			3rd Corps R.A. N° 2 &c 347 of 22/4/15	
	26/4/15		2/Lt Hoyt Evans returned from Dieppe. Lt Jackson U.S.A. (M.O.) reported for duty from 6th field	
			ambulance. Capt. W. Hodgson posted to the Command N° 2 Section	
	27/4/15		2/Lt A. Amey appointed Adjutant and to hold actual rank of Captain whilst so employed. (D.R.O. No.)	
			2/Lt P.H. Hoyt to Hospital sick.	
	28/4/15		2/Lt H.V. Evans attached 273 Bde and 42 other ranks.	
	29/4/15		C.R.A. visited S.A.A. Lines. 2/Lt C.V. Perrin to report from 23rd Bde. 2/Lt Kemp 236 Bde	
			attached D.A.H.Q. Lt Jackson U.S.A returned to 6th Field Ambulance.	
	30/4/15		Lt W.S.D. Marshall to R.A. Canteen. 1/L Fullerton for Staff learners course. 1st S. Lancasters attached 236 Bde	
			Lt J. Ballantyne and Cpl. Rev. G.H. Hayne to Hospital sick.	

A.H. Currie Capt. RFA
Acting Adj.

Army Form C. 2118.

47 D Am Col

9A 38

WAR DIARY
or
INTELLIGENCE SUMMARY.
(Erase heading not required.)

Instructions regarding War Diaries and Intelligence Summaries are contained in F. S. Regs., Part II. and the Staff Manual respectively. Title pages will be prepared in manuscript.

No. 1

Place	Date	Hour	Summary of Events and Information	Remarks and references to Appendices
Lompres Ste Marie	1/7/15		The C.R.A. inspected the Column, less S.A.A. Section	
	2/7/15		2/Lt H.G.Y. Whitty reported from E. & R.A.E.	
	3/7/15		The C.O. inspected Indian drivers in Driving Drill	
	"		2/Lt P.H. Hogg rejoined from hospital. 2/Lt C.V. Perrin reported from 235 Brigade. Lieut. Hing rejoined (att. 235 Brigade) transferred to 3rd Balloon Wing. S.O. strength 3/7/15	
	5/7/15		Lieut. E.T. Wingworth M.C. C/235 Battery, posted to N° 2 Section	
	"		Lieut. F.J. Stewart D/235 Battery, posted to command S.A.A. Section apt. to hold rank of Captain whilst so employed.	
	"		Lieut. C.R. Hollis N°1 Section att 236 Brigade posted to B/236 Battery	
	"		Lieut. E.A. De B. West D/236 Battery, posted to S.A.A. Section	
	"		2/Lt F. Ellowitz att 236 Brigade, posted to D/236 Battery	
	6/7/15		Capt. W. Hodgkinson proceeded on leave (8th to 22nd)	
	7/7/15		to Cullume to See Corres 3rd Corps clerk.	
	"		Lieut. H.S.E. Bushell reported from R.A. Section	
	"		Sgt Weedon to R.A. Section for instruction	

Army Form C. 2118.

WAR DIARY
or
INTELLIGENCE SUMMARY
(Erase heading not required.)

N° 2
6/7/18 to 13/7/18

Instructions regarding War Diaries and Intelligence Summaries are contained in F. S. Regs., Part II. and the Staff Manual respectively. Title pages will be prepared in manuscript.

Place	Date	Hour	Summary of Events and Information	Remarks and references to Appendices
Longpre to Amiens	6/7/18		2/Lt J.F. Crawford proceeded to report to C.R.A. Defence Commander at Vaux for two weeks attachment. Lieut L.C.B. Colthurst posted to 2/235 vice Lieut H. Stewart attached to S.A.A. Section. Lieut W.G.B. Thompson posted to 2/235 vice Lieut Illingworth.	
"	"		Balloon King.	
"	9/7/18		2/Lt E.D. Day reported from Base.	
"	10/7/15		2/Lt W.C.F. Miller proceeded to join 235 Brigade R.F.A.	
"	9/7/18		2/Lt F. Miller proceeded to join 236 Bde. Capt G.H. Wayne O.F. rejoined from Hospital. (Establishment &/8) Re-organisation Completed. Capt F.F. Steward joined S.A.A. Section. 3 Fire Alarms given (practice)	
"	11/7/18		2/Lt C.D. Day attached to 236 Brigade with effect from today. Lieut E.A. De B. West joined S.A.A. Section.	
"	12/7/18		S.A.A. Section moved to Montigny under orders issued by 47 Division "Q" B.M.A.I.O. (map M.2.D.) S.A.A. Dump taken over from 17 Division U.21 C.F.E. (Map 57D)	
"	13/7/15		2/Lt C.W. MacKinnon and 2 N.C.O's proceeded to Rouen for Indian Course. Column moved from Longpré (less S.A.A.) H.Q. to Beaucourt, N° 1 and 2 Sections	

Army Form C. 2118.

WAR DIARY
or
INTELLIGENCE SUMMARY.
(Erase heading not required.)

Instructions regarding War Diaries and Intelligence Summaries are contained in F. S. Regs., Part II. and the Staff Manual respectively. Title pages will be prepared in manuscript.

N° 3 13/7/18
23/7/18

Place	Date	Hour	Summary of Events and Information	Remarks and references to Appendices
LONGPRE	13/7/18		in vicinity of BAVELINCOURT.	
BEAUCOURT	14/7/18		Final location H.Q. T30 C.35.40. (Map 57D) N°1 Section C1 A 65.35. N° 2 Section C.L.D.24. (Map 62D). A.R.P. taken over at noon U21 A 65.20 (Map 57D)	
"	"		Lieut E.A.D.B. WEST attached 3rd Corps Reserve Depot.	
"	15/7/18		Sgt NEEDON reported from R.A. Section after one weeks attachment. 2/Lt A. CULLERNE from Gas Course and proceeded to join 236 Brigade for attachment.	
"	17/7/18		2/Lt C.V. PERRIN seen by a Medical Board.	
"	18/7/18		2/Lt C.V. PERRIN to Hospital, sick.	
"	19/7/18		R.S.M. proceeded on leave. 2/Lt J.C. SHERRIFFS and 2/Lt A.P. HENDERSON joined from Base.	
"	21/7/18		Lieut W.S.D. MARSHALL att'd 3rd Corps Gas School. Lieut M.H. HUGHES to A.R.P. for instruction 2/Lt HENDERSON & SHERRIFFS to 235 Brigade for attachment. 37 Remounts collected from Canal Bank.	
"	23/7/18		P.GOUIGNY, C.R.A. visited H.Q. and S.A.A. Section. Lieut E. CRUNDEN SMITH, General Lists joined. Rev Capt G.H. WAYNE to S.A.A.	

T2134. Wt. W708—776. 500000. 4/15. Sir J. C. & S.

Army Form C. 2118.

WAR DIARY
or
INTELLIGENCE SUMMARY.
(Erase heading not required.)

N° of 23/7/18 to 31/7/18

Instructions regarding War Diaries and Intelligence Summaries are contained in F.S. Regs., Part II. and the Staff Manual respectively. Title pages will be prepared in manuscript.

Place	Date	Hour	Summary of Events and Information	Remarks and references to Appendices
BEAUVOIS	23/7/18		Lieut R. LYELL joined from Base, 53 Reinforcements received.	
"	24/7/18		Capt. Hutchinson reported from leave.	
"	26/7/18		G.O.C. visited N° 1 & 2 Sections. Him at 5.30 pm.	
"	28/7/18		At about 1.30 am hostile aircraft dropped two bombs in close proximity to these H.Q.	
"	29/7/18		Lieut W.S.D. Marshall from Gas Course. Capt F.G. Stapley posted from B/235 Battery. Gunner SEARLES S.A.A. Section wounded by enemy shell fire whilst with Conv. on fatigues. 2/Lt Cantrect F.W. proceeded on leave to ROUEN (10 days).	
"	31/7/18		Hostile planes active during night, many bombs dropped.	

Harry Capt
for O.C. 7 S.B.

47th Divl. Artillery

47th DIVISIONAL AMMUNITION COLUMN

AUGUST 1918.

WAR DIARY or INTELLIGENCE SUMMARY

Army Form C. 2118.

No. 1

47/300
Vol 39

1/8/15 to 9/8/15

Place	Date	Hour	Summary of Events and Information	Remarks and references to Appendices
BEAUCOURT	1.8.15		At about 5 P.M. Hostile Planes fired at of our Observation Balloons.	
	2.8.15		Lt. M. MAROWITZ U.S.A. reported as Medical Officer from 6th Field Ambulance. 2/Lt H. BRAGG, posted from 235 Brigade R.F.A, and joined D.A.C. same date. 2/Lt T.J.J. CRAWFORD, posted to A.A. Defences.	
	3.8.15		Capt W.H.DICKINSON, R.A.M.C. proceeded on leave to U.K. 4/8/15 to 18/8/15.	
	4.8.15		Anniversary of Outbreak of War.	
	5.8.15		R.S.M. S.J. DENCHFIELD rejoined from Leave.	
	6.8.15		2/Lt H.E. FRAZER, attached 236 Brigade. Lt T. BALLANTYNE, rejoined from Hospital. 2/Lt C.T. HALL, 106 CHINESE LABOUR COMPANY reported for attachment to Battery, re his suitability for transfer to R.F.A. (Authority A.G. 2407/420 d/- 29/7/15.	
	7.8.15		Lt H. SPENCER reported from Base. Monthly Transport Competition held by C.O. Lt S.E. PIXLEY due to report from Base.	
	8.8.15		Attack made on 4th Army Front successful, all objectives reached. 2/Lt C.T. HALL, Labour Company to 235 Bde. R.F.A. Lt T. BALLANTYNE posted from S.A.A. Section to No. 2 Section.	
	9.8.15		Capt. F.G. STAPLEY reported.	

Army Form C. 2118.

WAR DIARY
or
INTELLIGENCE SUMMARY.

No. 2

9/8/18 to 15/8/18

(Erase heading not required.)

Instructions regarding War Diaries and Intelligence Summaries are contained in F. S. Regs., Part II. and the Staff Manual respectively. Title pages will be prepared in manuscript.

Place	Date	Hour	Summary of Events and Information	Remarks and references to Appendices
BEAUVOIRT	9/8/18		Hostile Planes over at about 11 P.M. Bombs dropped in No. 1 Section Lines. Casualties Lt R. LIELL one European O.R. and two Indian O.R. wounded, 19 mules killed, also one Rider, 2 Riders and 25 mules wounded.	
	10/8/18		2/Lt H.G.J. WHITBY attached to posted to D/235. 25 Remounts arrived (5 Riders 21 LD) 2 taken into M.V. Hospital, 1 destroyed. 2/Lt F.W. COWLAND rejoined from Leave in FRANCE. Lt K.V.H. MURRAY No 16 Yeomanry Att² 235 Bde. transferred to England (Authority A.9 N.A.B. 2407/29/(0) 2/8/18.	
	11/8/18		Capt F.G. STAPLEY reported to 142 Inf Bde H.Q. for 3 weeks probationary Staff Course. S.A.A. Section moved under 47 Div orders to I.7.A. (Map 62D Fins)	
	12/8/18		47 Div H.Q. & 47 D.A. H.Q. moved to HEILLY. 47 Div Artillery less H.Q. came under orders of 18 D.A. at 10 A.M. 2/Lt H.C.F. MILTON indentely boarded to England.	
	14/8/18		15 Wagon team from S.A.A. Section to Forward Dump at I.18.D.2.6. Lt M.H. WALKER M.C. att² 3rd Corps Reserve Depot.	
	15/8/18		C.O. and 2/Lt HOPE attended D.H.Q. B.S.M. MOSS, 1 B.Q.M.S, 1 SGT, and 1 Farrier Sgt. to Base Depot for Tour of Home Duty.	

Army Form C. 2118.

WAR DIARY
or
INTELLIGENCE SUMMARY.
(Erase heading not required.)

No. 3
16/8/15
to
24/8/15

Place	Date	Hour	Summary of Events and Information	Remarks and references to Appendices
BEAUCOURT	16/8/15		M.O. inspected water carts. ½ N°1 and 2 Sections and found them satisfactory. 14 Reinforcements received. 1 Rider and 19 L.D. received. D.A.R.O. advises that embarkation orders, re Lt. S.E. Pixley are cancelled.	
	17/8/15		Major H. Milvain 47 D.A. Horsemaster, is attached to these H.Qrs.	
	18/8/15		A.R.P. moved to D.2. A.5.3.	
	19/8/15		Lt E.A. de B. West rejoined from 2nd Corps Res. Dump.	
	20/8/15		Capt W.H. Dickinson R.A.M.C. rejoined from leave.	
	21/8/15		S.A.A. Section moved to I.15.d.2.6. 2/Lt G.W. MacKinnon rejoined from Rouen. Lt M. Marowitz M.R.C. U.S.A. returned to 6th Field Ambulance. 2/Lt W.L. Hope and Dr Keillard wounded, also 3 mules by Enemy Shell fire, on way to Guns.	
	22/8/15		Lt. T. Ballantyne proceeded on leave to U.K. 23rd to 6/9/15. E.A. bombing during night. 2/Lt A. Cullerne to Hospital (Jaundice) from 236 Bde.	
	23/8/15		Capt J. MacBride AVC to MVS for Duty. S.O. 47 D.A. moved with 15 D.A. to Hénencourt Château. 2/Lt Frazer att. 236 Bde. wounded.	
	24/8/15		N°2 Section moved to V19 A 9.4; N°1 Section new location V19 B 9.0. H.Q. new location V24 B.0.4.	

Army Form C. 2118.

WAR DIARY
or
INTELLIGENCE SUMMARY.

N°. 4

25/8/15 to 31/8/15

(Erase heading not required.)

Place	Date	Hour	Summary of Events and Information	Remarks and references to Appendices
MARLOY ALBERT	25/8/15		2/Lt F.E. INGHAM and Lt K. LIELL proceeded to 236 Bde. for attachment. Column moved to new area at E.3.C. S.W. of ALBERT. 2/Lt D.D. DAVIES and 2/Lt J.O. SHERREFFS att¹ 235 Bde wounded.	
	26/8/15		40 Remounts collected. S. Capt R.A. att² to these H.Qrs. One Indian D. wounded, and 2 Mules killed by live Grenade.	
	27/8/15		2/Lt A.W. WOOLLETT + 2/Lt H.M. HUGHES, proceeded to A/235 Bty for attachment. 40 Remounts handed over to 15 D.A.C. 2/Lt D.D. DAVIES, reported died of wounds. 2/Lt C.J.K. HILL joined from Base.	
	29/8/15 30/8/15		N°. 2 Section moved to F.4 A.5.2. (Sheet centered ALBERT) S.A.A. Section moved to F.4.C.30.10 Lt H. SPENCER posted to D/235 Bty. Lt M.M. FIRTH, joined from Base. Lt M.H. WALKER M.C. rejoined from 3ʳᵈ Corps Reserve Dumps. H.Q. + N°. 1 Section moved to new area. H.Q. F.4.C.0.4. N°.1 F¹ᵈ A.5.5.	
FRICOURT	31/8/15		2/Lt's W.W. USHER, and H.G. HAMMOND rejoined from Trench Mortars. Lt H. SPENCER proceeded to join D/235 Bty	

A. Young Capt.
A/Aq. 47 Divn

Army Form C. 2118.

WAR DIARY
or
INTELLIGENCE SUMMARY.
(Erase heading not required.)

N° 1. 47 DAC 1st Sept 1915
8/9/15

N° 40

Place	Date	Hour	Summary of Events and Information	Remarks and references to Appendices
FRICOURT	1/9/15		Capt. Rev. G.H. Wayne C.F. proceeded on Leave (2nd to 16th)	
"	2/9/15		N° 1 Section moved to B.I.D.S.S. N° 2 Section moved to S.24.B.5.9. Sections working under Brigade Column B.A.C.	
"	3/9/15		N° 2 Section moved to T.29.C.4.11. N° 1 Section moved to B.5.C.5.8.	
MONTAUBAN	4/9/15		H.Q. moved to A.4.R.5.4. (MONTAUBAN) 47 DIV ARTILLERY administered by 47 DIVISION. Sections D.A.C. came under Command of O.C. 47 D.A.C. Lt M.H. WALKER M.C. posted to B/235 Bty with effect from today. Joined Bty 13.9.15	
"	5/9/15		S.A.A. Section moved to H.3 Central. S.E. HEMMWOOD. N° 2 Section moved to B.4.C.7.5.	
"	6/9/15		25 Reinforcements received. Lt C.E. WILES reported from ENGLAND.	
"	7/9/15		MAJOR R. McILVAIN returned to 47 D.A. Division relieved in Line. Whole Column moved to MERICOURT L'ABBE. Lt M.H. WALKER rejoined from 235 Bde. 2/Lt C.R. CONYERS attached 235 Bde posted to B/235 Battery	
MERICOURT L'ABBE	8/9/15		Lt R. LIELL B/236 Bty transferred to ENGLAND. Column proceeded to Entraining Station. Gun Section detailed 16.G. + 4 D.F. Wagons to travel with each Bty. Remainder of N° 1 Section Entrained with 235 Bde H.Q.	

WAR DIARY or INTELLIGENCE SUMMARY

Army Form C. 2118.

N° 2
8/9/15
to
13/9/15

Place	Date	Hour	Summary of Events and Information	Remarks and references to Appendices
MERICOURT L'ABBÉ	8/9/15		Remainder of N° 2 Section travelled with 236 Bde H.Q. from HEILLY at 3.45 A.M.	
	9/9/15		9/9/15 to CHOCQUES. Half S.A.A. Section travelled with X/47 T.M.B. from MERICOURT at 7.38 am 9/9/15 to LILLERS. Half S.A.A. Section travelled with Y/47 T.M.B at 10.35 A.M. 9/9/15 from MERICOURT to LILLERS. H.Q. travelled with N°1 Company DIV TRAIN, by road close to liaison at 6.45 A.M. 9th from HEILLY to CHOCQUES. All store timings are those laid down in 47 D.A. administrative Instructions. H.Q. left HEILLY STATION at 11 A.M. and arrived at CHOCQUES at 7.15 P.M. Branched to AMES arriving at about midnight. Whole Column billeted in AMES.	
AMES	10/9/15			
	12/9/15		DIVISION transferred to 13 CORPS 5th ARMY. 4 G.S. Wagon + team attached to 42 A.T. Coy R.E. at Lonney for duty. LT G.H. NEVILL B/235 Bty posted to Command N°1 Section, joined Column 13/9/15. 2/CAPT H.J.GLOVER transferred to B/235 Bty as reserve to Lt Young Bty 13/9/15. 2/Lt H.J. EVANS posted as Orderly Officer 235 Bde R.F.A. Lt C.E. WILLES attached N° 2 Section, posted to B/236 Bty joined Battery 13/9/15. LT M.M. FIRTH 2/Lt R.H. HOGG 2/Lt H. SHEPHERD to be attached 235 Bde R.F.A. joined Bde. 13/9/15.	
	13/9/15		C.R.A. visited Column. Lt C.S. JACQUES joined from Base. Lt R.A. COATES	

Army Form C. 2118.

WAR DIARY
or
INTELLIGENCE SUMMARY.

(Erase heading not required.)

N° 3

13/9/18
2/9/18
20/9/18

Instructions regarding War Diaries and Intelligence Summaries are contained in F. S. Regs., Part II. and the Staff Manual respectively. Title pages will be prepared in manuscript.

Place	Date	Hour	Summary of Events and Information	Remarks and references to Appendices
AMIENS	13/9/18		LT. O. EDWARDS posted to N° 2 Section, but not yet reported.	
	14/9/18		N° 2 Section moved under orders from 19th D.A. to N° 3 & D.E.Q. for Salvage Work. 86 L.D. HORSES received and posted to R.H.A. Section, 42 Mules to 236 Bde. and 44 Mules to 236 Bde. Temporary exchange. 10 G.S. Wagons and Teams under 2/Lt MACKINNON moved forward to Lines next to N°2 Section for work under 52 Heavy Bty. R.G.A.	
	15/9/18		2/Lt H.G. HAMMOND and 5 O.R. proceeded to 1st ARMY T.M. Course.	
	16/9/18		Major H.H. POLLOCK M.C. proceeded on Leave 17 to 1.10.18.	
	17/9/18		2/Lt L.G. SAMS with 47 Div Signals posted to 186 Bde R.G.A. C.R.A. visited. Orders received to move to MARLES. Cancelled at later hour.	
	18/9/18		LT. O. EDWARDS, M.C. reported. 2/Lt C.G.G. MENHAM, R.B.M. WILKINS and W.J. CAPERN reported from Base. LT. W.S.D. MARSHALL to 47 D.A.H.Q. G.O.C. R.A.13th CORPS visited Column. 42 Reinforcement arrived.	
	19/9/18		N° 2 Section reported from 19th D.A. Party rejoined from 52 Heavy Bty R.G.A. Reinforcement to Brigades 26 to 235 and 31 to 236 Bde. Column moved from AMIENS, to MARLES leaving old lines at 11.15 A.M.	

Army Form C. 2118.

WAR DIARY
or
INTELLIGENCE SUMMARY.
(Erase heading not required.)

N° 4
20/9/15
to
30/9/15

Place	Date	Hour	Summary of Events and Information	Remarks and references to Appendices
MAREST	21/9/15		4 Reinforcements received 3 E/r 235 and 6 L/r 236.	
"	24/9/15		Orders reference entrainment postponed. Lt. R.A. COATES proceeded to report to A.A.D.C. 3rd ARMY for attachment and proceeded to A.A. Battery	
"			Capt. Rev G.H. WAYNE rejoined from leave.	
"			During stay at MAREST all preparations made to pack and prepare stores for handing over.	
"			Training was also carried out.	
"	26/9/15		Capt. F.J. STEWARD proceeded to leave via CALAIS.	
"	27/9/15		Column moved to ANVIN leaving MAREST at 11.20 A.M. arriving at destination at about 3.30 P.M. G.O.C. Div and Column en Route.	
ANVIN				
"	28/9/15		C.R.A. awaited here.	
"	29/9/15		B.S.M. FREEMAN reported.	

A. Hunt Capt.
Adjutant R.E.

47 D Am Col

No 1.
1/10/18
to 6/10/18

WAR DIARY
or
INTELLIGENCE SUMMARY.
(Erase heading not required.)

Army Form C. 2118.

Place	Date	Hour	Summary of Events and Information	Remarks and references to Appendices
AMES	1/10/18		Column moved from ANVIN leaving at 12.00 hrs to AMES arriving there at about 16.00 hrs.	
ROBECQ	2/10/18		Column moved from AMES at 10.30 hrs to P.28.a.2.1 Sheet 36.A. on ROBECQ Rd arriving at 15.00 hrs	
LA GORGUE	3/10/18		Column moved to L.35.a.5.4. LA GORGUE nr ESTAIRES. Maj H.H. POLLOCK MC rejoined from leave. Wagon Lines etc. took over from Sq D.A.C. A.P.P. taken over at R.3.C.6.7 (LESTREM). Lieut (A/capt) W.P. BOULTON & Lieut P. BEW posted & attached XI Bde.	
LAVENTIE	4/10/18		Column less S.A.A. Section moved to new lines at Iy 36.d.0.4. (Sheet 36) N.E. of LAVENTIE. S.A.A. Section to N.7.d.7.1 maps sides from Div. O.Q. Ammunition supplied since 12.00 hrs A.15.44 AX.144 & BX.656 BS.45	
—	5/10/18		Ammunition supplied to 12.00 hrs 6th A.396 AX.1068 BX.744	
—	6/10/18		Lieut F.C. INGRAM proceeded on leave (7 to 21/10/18). 2/Lieut F.W. COWARD proceeded to U.K. for four home duty (Auth A.G.63.09) Ammunition issued to 12.00 hrs 7th A.884 AX.556 BX.130	

Army Form C. 2118.

WAR DIARY
or
INTELLIGENCE SUMMARY.
(Erase heading not required.)

No. 2 7/10/18 to 14/10/18

Place	Date	Hour	Summary of Events and Information	Remarks and references to Appendices
LA VENTIE	7/10/18		Ammunition issued to 8th A276 AX228 BX296.	
—	8/10/18		do do do do 9th A126 AX126.	
—	9/10/18		do do do do 10th A252 AX228 BX588	
—	10/10/18		do do do do 11th A632 AX227 BX576	
—	11/10/18		2/Lieut J.M. McDOUALL joined from Base. 42 mules from 235 + 44 from 236 Bdes, exchanged for similar number in column. Ammunition issued to 12.00 hrs 12th A568 AX608 BX588	
—	12/10/18	12.00 hrs	2/Lieut T.S. CARR rejoined from Base. Ammunition issued to 13th A1632 AX760 BX588.	
—	13/10/18		2/Lieut H. BRAGG proceeded on leave via CALAIS (period 14-28/10/18) Capt F.J. STEWARD rejoined from leave. Ammunition issued to 12.60 hrs 14th A765 AX299 BX588	
—	14/10/18		Lieut E A de B WEST proceeded on leave via CALAIS (period 15th 29/10/18) G.O.C. R.A. XI Corps visited H.Q. +1+2 Secs. Ammunition issued to 12.00 hrs 15th A784 AX632.	

Army Form C. 2118.

WAR DIARY
or
INTELLIGENCE SUMMARY.
(Erase heading not required.)

N° 3   15/10/18
       25/10/18

Instructions regarding War Diaries and Intelligence Summaries are contained in F. S. Regs., Part II. and the Staff Manual respectively. Title pages will be prepared in manuscript.

Place	Date	Hour	Summary of Events and Information	Remarks and references to Appendices
LAVENTIE	15/10/18		All available teams out on Salvage work. Ammunition salved to date from rounds 18 Pdr. 5705. 4.5"How 2167. 6" 1508 do dr 532	
—	16/10/18		All available teams out on salvage work. Ammunition Salved 18 Pdr 2457. 4.5" How 658. B.S.M. SHELLEY proceeded on leave (17 to 31/10/18)	
—	17/10/18		2/Lieut G.C. JOHNSTON reported. Ammunition Salved 4.5" How 729	
ST FLORIS	18/10/18		Column relieved by 57 DAC & moved at 09.30 hrs to ST FLORIS (P6a.1.0. Sheet 62A)	
—	19/10/18		Lieut (a/Capt) W.P. BOULTON & Lieut P. BEN transferred to 57 D.A.	
—	20/10/18		2/Lieut H.G. HAMMOND proceeded on leave (21/10/18 - 4/11/18) via CALAIS	
—	21/10/18		2/Lieut T.S. CARR & party proceeded to collect remounts	
—	22/10/18		Lieut F.C. INGRAM rejoined from leave.	
—	23/10/18		R.O. inspected men & harness of Column. 45 Remounts collected	
BOUT DEVILLE	25/10/18		Capt. A. LAMY proceeded on leave (26/10/18 - 9/11/18). Column moved from ST FLORIS at 09.00 hrs to BOUT DEVILLE (R24 a 6.7. Sheet 36A) arriving at latter place at about 13.00 hrs	

Army Form C. 2118.

WAR DIARY
INTELLIGENCE SUMMARY.
(Erase heading not required.)

No 14   26/10/18 to 31/10/18

Place	Date	Hour	Summary of Events and Information	Remarks and references to Appendices
HAUBOURDIN	28/10/18		Column moved from BOUT DEVILLE at 08.00 hrs & arrived at HAUBOURDIN (S.W. of LILLE) at about 14.00 hrs. 2/Lieut B.F. PAUL reported from 1/47 TMB & Att'chd 235 Bde R.F.A. 2/Lieut W.W. USHER att'chd 235 Bde R.F.A. Lieut C.S. JAQUES att'chd 236 Bde R.F.A. 2/Lieut H.G. HAMMOND post'd to 1/47 TMB (at present on leave). 2/Lieut C.J.K. HILL post'd to X/47 TMB. 2/Lieuts T.S. CARR & J.H. McDOUALL att'chd to 47 TMBs.	
LE BREUCQ	28/10/18		47 Div. marched through LILLE on occasion of 5th Army Commander presenting his standard to the Major. D.A.C. represented by 2.0 Adjt. Section & commanders & 10 teams & vehicles. Column marched from HAUBOURDIN at 16.00 to LE BREUCQ (LESART ans) arriving at 14.15 hrs.	
—	29/10/18		G.O.C. Div. inspected round lines.	
—	30/10/18		2.0 & Adjt reconnoitred new lines.	
—	31/10/18		SAA Section moved under orders from 47 Div Q to M6d.5.5 (LE MOUSCRON) & relieved SAA Sec. 57 DAC.	

F.C. Ingham ? Major RFA
O.C. 47 DAC

Army Form C. 2118.

N° 1   1st November to 7th November

47 D Aus Col

9/3/4

WAR DIARY
or
INTELLIGENCE SUMMARY.
(Erase heading not required.)

Instructions regarding War Diaries and Intelligence Summaries are contained in F. S. Regs., Part II. and the Staff Manual respectively. Title pages will be prepared in manuscript.

Place	Date	Hour	Summary of Events and Information	Remarks and references to Appendices
BREUGP	1.11.15		H.Qr, 1 and 2 Sections moved from BREUEG at 1000 hrs and arrived at LA GRAND MARAIS at 1230 hrs, and relieved H.Q and Sections of 57 D.A.C. Location H.Q M4C2.2. N°1 M4C3.3. N°2 M4A5.3. Sheet 37 1/40000. LIEUT E.A. DE B. WEST and 2/LT H. BRAGG rejoined from Leave. Ammunition delivered to 1030 2nd Nov. A758 AX722 BX944	
	2.11.15		HAVILDAR MAJOR CHANAN SINGH proceeded to Indian Base Depot ROVEN reference Commission. Ammunition issued to 1030 hrs 3rd Nov. A266 AX366 BX312.	
	3.11.15		Ammunition issued to 1030 hrs 4th Nov A100 AX152 BX312	
	4.11.15		N°1 Section moved to new lines at M.16 D.5.4. Ammunition issued to 1030 hrs 5th Nov A.128 AX200 BX192	
	5.11.15		Ammunition issued to 1030 hrs 6 Nov A.136 AX.136.	
	6.11.15		LT W.S.D. MARSHALL rejoined from 47 D.A. H.Q. N°1 Section moved to 1030 7th Nov A.190 AX214 BX 240. 24 Remounts arrived. Ammunition issued to Mg A00.20. 2/LT HAMMOND arrived from Leave.	
	7.11.15		2/LT HAMMOND proceeded to join T.M. Bty.	

Army Form C. 2118.

No. 2

WAR DIARY
or
INTELLIGENCE SUMMARY.
(Erase heading not required.)

7 Nov to 15/11/15

Instructions regarding War Diaries and Intelligence Summaries are contained in F. S. Regs., Part II. and the Staff Manual respectively. Title pages will be prepared in manuscript.

Place	Date	Hour	Summary of Events and Information	Remarks and references to Appendices
BREUCQ	7.11.15		2/Lt R.M.B. WILKINS and W.J. CAPERN to Hospital, sick. Ammunition issued to 1030 hrs 8th A608 AX760 BX 342.	
	8.11.15		D.D.R. 5th ARMY held parade of animals for Casting. Ammunition issued to 1030. 9th A Nll AX 325.	
	9.11.15		16 Reinforcements received. D.A.R.O. of today shew following posting 2/Lt R.T. COLTHURST att'd C/235- Brigade to C/235- 27/9/15. 2/Lt P.H. HOGG att'd 235 Brigade to A/235- 24/10/15. 2/Lt H.M. HUGHES att'd 235 Bde to D/235- 11/10/15. S.A.A. SECTION moved to BLANDAIN, N10 D.8.2.	
	10.11.15		Column, less S.A.A. moved to new area at FOURERUIX. Location H.Q. N6. B.J.8. No 1 N.5.D.8.3. No 2 N.6. A. 15.05. S.A.A. moved to CHAT-DE-BREUGE J34 C.3.9.	
FOURERUIX	11.11.15		CAPT. A. LAMY rejoined from Leave. 2/Lt W.J. CAPERN from Hospital. SAA Section moved to N.2.B.4.7. Hostilities ceased at 1100 hrs.	
	12.11.15		LT G.W. MACKINNON att'd D.H.Q. Educational Officer.	
	15.11.15		LT G.W. MACKINNON appointed Educational Officer 47th DIV and S.O.S. Column moved to LOUVIL Area, leaving old lines at 1015 hrs and arriving at destination at 1345 hrs. Location H.Q. S.20.C.4.0. No1 B.25- B.57. No 2 S.20 A 5.4. S.A.A. S.21. A.9.0. (CYSOING)	

Army Form C. 2118.

WAR DIARY
or
INTELLIGENCE SUMMARY.

(Erase heading not required.)

N: 3

16 Nov to 30/11/18

Instructions regarding War Diaries and Intelligence Summaries are contained in F. S. Regs., Part II. and the Staff Manual respectively. Title pages will be prepared in manuscript.

Place	Date	Hour	Summary of Events and Information	Remarks and references to Appendices
LOUVIL	16.11.18		C.R.A. visited Lines. 48 Remounts received. N:1 Section moved to S.15.A.75.40 (CYSOING.) 2/Lt H.E. FRAZER reported. 33 Reinforcements received.	
	17.11.18		C.R.A. attended Section Church Parade.	
	19.11.18		30 Teams out transporting Ammunition from A.R.P.3 to A.S.C.Q Railhead.	
	22.11.18		Detached Teams and personnel on Ammunition work reported. LT.M.S.D. MARSHALL to 235: Bde as a/adjt.	
	24.11.18		Capt G.H. NEVILL proceeded on leave 25/11 to 9/12/18 Via Cal. 413. LIEUT E. ARUNDEL SMITH to Hospl. Hav. Major CHANAN SINGH rejoined from RUEN.	
	27.11.18		Column moved from LOUVIL and CYSOING at 0700 hrs and arrived at FOURNES at 13.45 hrs.	
FOURNES	28.11.18		Column moved from FOURNES at 07.50 and arrived at CHOCQUES at 15.00 hrs.	
	30/11/18		G.O.C. DIVISION inspected Lines and Billets of the Column.	

A Young Capt
Capt & OC.

WAR DIARY or INTELLIGENCE SUMMARY

Army Form C. 2118.

47D Am Col

N:1
4.12.18
29.12.18

Place	Date	Hour	Summary of Events and Information	Remarks and references to Appendices
CHOCQUES	4.12.18		2/Lt R.B.M. WILKINS reports from Hospital.	
-"-	7/12/18		2/Lt S.S. ENGLISH reports from BASE	
-"-	11/12/18		Capt G.H. NEVILL rejoined from leave.	
-"-	"		2/Lt R.B.M. WILKINS proceeded to CORPS CONCENTRATION CAMP as Contracting Officer	
-"-	"		with MINERS for Discharge.	
-"-	"		Leave granted to 2/Lt R.B.M. WILKINS 17th to 31st. 41 Reinforcements received.	
-"-	13.12.18		Lt W.S.D. MARSHALL and 235 BdR proceeded on leave 14 to 28th	
-"-	"		9 Animals paraded at HESDIGNEUL Common, for Inspection by Corps	
-"-	"		HORSEMASTER, also 7 Bord Mares.	
-"-	16.12.18		G.O.C and B.G.R.A. visited Column.	
-"-	17.12.18		CAPT CARLTON R.A.M.C. for A.D.M.S. visited and inspected Camp.	
-"-	21.12.18		CAPT W. HODGKINSON proceeded on leave to U.K. 21st to 4th 1915.	
-"-	26.12.18		G.O.C. DIVISION visited H.Q.	
-"-	29.12.18		Lt W.S.D. MARSHALL rejoined from leave.	

A. [signature] Capt
Adj 47 D.A.C.

WAR DIARY
or
~~INTELLIGENCE SUMMARY~~
(Erase heading not required.)

Army Form C. 2118.

N° 1   1st to 19th   47 Bde

Place	Date	Hour	Summary of Events and Information	Remarks and references to Appendices
CHOCQUES	1/1/19		Lt Col Cossart D.S.O. A/C.R.A. visited Column.	
"	"		Lt L.B. Tansley posted from 236 Brigade. Lt C.S. Jaques posted B/216 Bty vice Lt L.B Tansley.	
"	2/1/19		2/Lt R.B.M. Wilkins returned from Leave.	
"	3/1/19		Capt Rev. G.H. Wayne C.F. left to join 47 Div Infantry	
"	4/1/19		Lt S.W.D. Marshall attached 235th Bde, for temporary duty.	
"	5/1/19		Veterinary Board classified Headquarters and N°2 Section animals.	
"	9/1/19		Veterinary Board classified N°1 Section Animals.	
"			Capt W.H. Dickinson R.A.M.C. proceeded on Leave, due to embark on 10th.	
"	10/1/19		Veterinary Board Classified Sea Section animals.	
"	14/1/19		2nd Remount Officer re-grouped animals of H.Q°, N°1 and Sea Section R.F.A.	
"	15/1/19		2/Lt T.S. Carr attached from T.M. to 236 Bde.	
"	16/1/19		13 Riders 21 L.D animals despatched to N°4 Base Remount Depôt	
"	17/1/19		10 Riders 30 LD animals despatched to N°4 Base Remount Depôt.	
"	18/1/19		Lt S.W.D. Marshall rejoined from 235 Bde.	
"	19/1/19		2/Lt T.S. Carr rejoined from 236th Bde – 2/Lt J. Miller posted to 235 Bde.	

WAR DIARY
or
INTELLIGENCE SUMMARY

Army Form C. 2118.

N° 2   19th to 31st

(Erase heading not required.)

Instructions regarding War Diaries and Intelligence Summaries are contained in F.S. Regs., Part II. and the Staff Manual respectively. Title pages will be prepared in manuscript.

Place	Date	Hour	Summary of Events and Information	Remarks and references to Appendices
CHOCQUES	20/1/19		Major H.H. POLLOCK M.C. proceeded on Leave (due to embark 22nd) Command Column. Lt F.A. de B. WEST Commands S.A.A. Section. Capt F.J. STEWARD T.M. Bn joined Column for duty (1 Officer & 9 other Ranks)	
"	22/1/19		3 Rivers 15 LD despatched HQ to Base Remount Depot.	
"	24/1/19		2/Lt H.F. FRAZER left unit en route to England and demobilization, and S.O.S.	
"	25/1/19		2/Lt C.L. THOMPSON struck off Strength.	
"	26/1/19		Capt W.H. DICKINSON reported from Leave in U.K.	
"	27/1/19		2/Lt R.B.M. WILKINS proceeded to D.R.C. en route for England and demobilization and S.O.S. 2/Lt H. BRAGG posted to N° 2 Section from S.A.A. Section Lt J.C.P. Brown joined from England, posted to D.A.C. and attached to S.A.H.Q.	
"	31/1/19		67 Class animals despatched HQ to Base Remount Depot.	

A. Hoop Capt
Actg D.A.C.

FEBRUARY. 1919.

WAR DIARY
or
INTELLIGENCE SUMMARY.

Army Form C. 2118.

47 D.A.C.

WD 45

Reference map BETHUNE Combined Sheet (36A.SE. 36 S.W. 36.B. NE. 36c. NW.)

Place	Date	Hour	Summary of Events and Information	Remarks and references to Appendices
CHOCQUES	Feb.1.		XI Corps C.R.A. visited Divisional Ammunition Column.	
	Feb.2nd		2/Lt A.A. SMITH posted to B/236 Battery.	
			2/Lt J. CHEYNE posted to C/236 Battery	
			2/Lt J.H. McDOUALL, T.M.B's, attached to No.1.Section for duty.	
			2/Lt F.C. INGRAM promoted acting captain and posted to command No.1 Section vice a/captain G.H. NEVILL.	
	Feb.3rd		Captain G.H. NEVILL proceeded to Divisional Reception Camp for demobilization, and was struck off strength of D.A.C.	
			2/Lt W.J. CAPEAN proceeded to Divisional Reception Camp as O/c Dispersal Draft.	
			D.A.D.R. visited and re-classified animals of D.A.C.	
	Feb.5th		C.R.A. 47th Divisional Artillery visited D.A.C.	
	Feb.9th		C.R.A. 47th Divisional Artillery visited Nos 1.&2. Sections.	

FEBRUARY, 1919.   47 D.A.C.   2.

Army Form C. 2118.

WAR DIARY
or
INTELLIGENCE SUMMARY.
(Erase heading not required.)

Instructions regarding War Diaries and Intelligence Summaries are contained in F.S. Regs., Part II. and the Staff Manual respectively. Title pages will be prepared in manuscript.

Place	Date	Hour	Summary of Events and Information	Remarks and references to Appendices
CHOCQUES	Feb. 12th		2/Lt W.J. CAPERN'S leave commences. (Period of leave Feb. 12 to 26).	Reference sheet BETHUNE (36A.SE, 36SW 36B, NE. 36c, NW) combined sheet
	Feb. 14th		2/Lt G.C. JOHNSTON and N.C.O.'s proceeded to MARSEILLES to collect 25 Indian O.R.'s.	
	Feb. 15th		Lt. J.H. McDOVALL proceeded on leave to U.K. (Period of leave Feb. 15 to 29).	
	Feb. 17th		A/Captain A. LAMY proceeded to BARLIN to take charge of XI Corps Animal Collecting Camp. Lt W.S.D. MARSHALL assumed duties of Acting Adjutant of D.A.C.	
	Feb. 18th		A/Captain D. EDWARDS, M.C. proceeded on leave to U.K. (Period of leave Feb. 18 to March 4).	
	Feb. 20th		A/Capt. W. HODGKINSON departed to obtain clearance certificates and remained two nights.	
	Feb. 21st		R.S.M. DENCHFIELD to hospital.	

Army Form C. 2118.

WAR DIARY
or
INTELLIGENCE SUMMARY.
(Erase heading not required.)

47. D.A.C.

Reference Map BETHUNE
contained sheet [36A.S.E. 36 S.W.
36B.N.E. 36C.N.W.

Place	Date	Hour	Summary of Events and Information	Remarks and references to Appendices
CHOCQUES	Feb. 22nd		Major H.H. POLLOCK. M.C. rejoined from leave.	
	24th		A/Captain F.J. STEWARD resumed command of S.A.A. Section. 6 L.D. horses and 24 L.D. mules despatched to XI Corps A.C.C. BARLIN for disposal to ROUEN: all 2 animals.	
	25th		R.S.M. BENCHFIELD rejoined from hospital. Lt. F.P. JAMES rejoined from leave.	
	27th		2/Lt H. BRAGG proceeded to take charge of LAPUGNOY Ammunition Dump. 28 horses and 22 mules despatched to LILLERS for issue on March 1st.	
	28th		2/Lt W.J. CAPERN rejoined from leave.	

H Marshall H.H.J.A.(J)
A/Adjt 47.D.A.C.

WAR DIARY or INTELLIGENCE SUMMARY

Army Form C. 2118.

47th D.A.C.

March 1919

Place	Date	Hour	Summary of Events and Information	Remarks and references to Appendices
CHOCQUES.	March 1st		161 Animals despatched to BARLIN, en route for No 4. Base Depot. 5 Animals sold at LILLERS.	Reference trench sheet BETHUNE continued. 36A.S.E. 36SW. 36B.NE. 36.N.W.
"	March 2nd		6 Riders to Base.	
"	" 3rd		Lt. J.H. McDOUALL rejoined LAPUGNOY supply dump from leave.	
"	" 4th		Lt. C. ELLIS joined from 1st Army School of Instrn.	
"	" 5th		Major H.H. POLLOCK.M.C. to Hospital.	
"	"		A/Captain F.J. STEWARD assumed command of D.A.C.	
"	"		A/Capt. O. EDWARDS rejoined from leave.	
"	"		Capt. W.H. DICKINSON. R.A.M.C. Left to join 6th (London) Field ambulance.	
"	" 7th		Lieut. C.A. MURAG. M.C. joined D.A.C. from 1st Army School of Instrn.	
"	March 8th		C.A.D. 47th D.A.C visited the D.A.C. and presented Transport Cup won by No 1 Section.	
"	" 10th		2/Lt T.S. CARR proceeded on leave (Period March 10-24)	
"	" 11th		83 Animals, 2 Lorries, transferred from 235 & 236 Brigades to D.A.C. 45 to No 1 Section.	
"	"		38 to No 2 Section.	
"	March 13th		84 animals despatched for Corps at LILLERS.	
"	" 14th		Lieut T. ELLIS proceeded on leave (Authy 1st Army L/3879) period March 15-24.	

WAR DIARY
or
INTELLIGENCE SUMMARY.
(Erase heading not required.)

Army Form C. 2118.

47 D.A.C.

March 1919

Instructions regarding War Diaries and Intelligence Summaries are contained in F.S. Regs, Part II. and the Staff Manual respectively. Title pages will be prepared in manuscript.

Place	Date	Hour	Summary of Events and Information	Remarks and references to Appendices
CHOCQUES	March 18		16 Animals despatched to BARLIN Camp en route for ENGLAND via No. 1. Base Remount Depot.	Antenna Mast Shed BETHUNE combined 36A.S.E. 36S.W. 36 B.N.E. 36.N.W.
"	" 19		2/Lt H.BRACE rejoined from LAPUGNOY Ammunition Dump. 4 Drivers despatched to Base.	
"	" 20		2/Lt S.S. ENGLISH proceeded on tour to YPRES. 4 Animals sold at BRUAY.	
"	" 21st		a/Captain D.EDWARDS. M.C. 2/Lt C.B.MENHAM left D.A.C. with the INDIANS for 2nd Division.	
"	"		Bdr ROUEN rejoined BARLIN. 2/Lt J.H. McDOUALL left for ROUEN.	
"	"		78 Animals to Base. Two Riding Cobs at BRUAY.	
"	22		2/Lt S.S. ENGLISH rejoined from tour to YPRES.	
"	25		Major General Sir A.E. GOARAINGE, G.O.C. 47 Division said farewell to D.A.C. on mounted parade.	
"	"		a/Capt. G.K. MACKINNON posted to D.A.C. from Divisional H.Q.	
"	"		30 L.D. Animals despatched to Base. 4 C.B. mules to 235 Brigade, 4/6 236 Brigade.	
"	26th		C.S.M. A. 47 D.A.C. Bmbr General E.K.WHITLEY. C.B. C.M. & D.S.O. paid farewell visit to D.A.C.	
"	"		2/Lt W.J. CABEAN and 2/Lt H.BRACE left for demobilization.	
"	27th		a/Capt F.J. STEWARD proceeded on leave (March 28 - April 11). a/Lt E.C. INGRAM resumed command of D.A.C. 13 L.D. Animals despatched to Base.	
"	30th		Lieut C. ELLIS rejoined from leave.	

H.S.Marshall Capt RFA(T)
a/Adjt 47 D.A.C.